Piano · Vocal

THE *Franz Waxman* COLLECTION

M-G-M FANFARE

Music by FRANZ WAXMAN

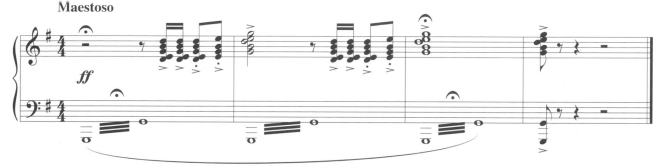

Franz Waxman composing "M-G-M Fanfare" at the
M.G.M. Studios, 1936. MGM photo by Carpenter.

Editor: Patrick Russ

On the cover: Franz Waxman in his music room, Los Angeles, CA, 1960. Photo by his son, John W. Waxman. The Oscar statuettes seen in the background are for his scores for *Sunset Boulevard* (1950) and *A Place in the Sun* (1951). A painting commissioned by the US Postal Service and based on this photo was used for the Franz Waxman commemorative stamp issued September 19, 1999.

ISBN 978-1-4950-2829-8

HAL•LEONARD®
7777 W. BLUEMOUND RD. P.O. BOX 13819 MILWAUKEE, WI 53213

Visit Hal Leonard Online at
www.halleonard.com

Franz Waxman: AN INTRODUCTION

My father, Franz Waxman, was born December 24, 1906 in the German coal mining town of Konigshutte (King's Hut) in Upper Silesia (now Chorzow, Poland). He was the youngest of eight children, six boys and two girls, in the family of Otto and Rosalie Perl Wachsmann, both of German Jewish descent. Otto was in the raw materials business while Rosalie was a part-time bookkeeper. Father's eldest brother Paul (1895–1982) played violin. His brother Max (1898–1918), who died during the last days of World War I, just before reaching his 20th birthday, was an artist interested in music. My father was a gifted pianist, but he entered the Berlin Conservatory in 1927 at the relatively late age of twenty-one. Like all students, he needed to supplement his income, so he got a job playing four-hand piano arrangements—with Bruno Walter's daughter, Gretel, no less!—at the Tingle-Tangle Club. His big break came when the club's owner, composer Friedrich Hollaender, asked him to orchestrate and conduct his score for the Marlene Dietrich/Joseph Von Sternberg film *The Blue Angel* (1930) at the UFA Studios. This assignment led to more work over the next three years composing and conducting scores for musicals such as *Paprika* and *Scampolo*.

About this time, Marlene Dietrich, who would become the leading German cabaret singer of her generation, commissioned my father and Max Colpet to compose—overnight!—"Alone in a Big City," which became one of her best-known hits. They wrote the song in a taxi between Dietrich's house and their hotel. At the same time, her French counterpart, Suzy Solidor, recorded Father's "La Belle Croisière (Magic Voyage)" (lyrics by Louis Poterat).

In the spring of 1934, while walking home from a recording session, Father was assaulted on the streets of Berlin by Nazi thugs. He picked himself up and, together with his friend, Alice Pauline Schachmann (1905–1957), immediately left Germany for Paris. While in France, he composed songs for the musical *La Crise est Finie*. The delightful German and French songs from this early period of my father's career, represented in this collection with English lyrics by Jeremy Lawrence, capture for me the nostalgic charm and sophistication of this bygone era. Other refugees from Berlin's UFA Studios soon joined my parents at the Ansonia Hotel in Paris, including directors Billy Wilder and Robert Siodmak, actor Peter Lorre, and former head of production Erich Pommer. Pommer was lucky enough to make a deal with 20th Century Fox in Hollywood to produce a film adaptation of the Jerome Kern/Oscar Hammerstein II show *Music in the Air*. He brought many former UFA colleagues, including Wilder and my father, to Los Angeles to work on the production. By 1934 my father had completed the musical adaptation of the Kern score for the film and had married Alice.

In 1935 Father joined Universal Pictures in Hollywood. His first score, *The Bride of Frankenstein*, made such an impact that he was promoted to Music Director. He was just twenty-nine. One of the first songs he wrote in America was "Something in My Heart" (lyrics by E.Y. Harburg) sung by Zasu Pitts on *The Affair of Susan* soundtrack. Although

thrilled with his new life in the United States, Father longed to compose full time and no longer wished to be saddled with the responsibilities of a music director. In 1936 he accepted an invitation to join the Metro-Goldwyn-Mayer music department as staff composer. Here he wrote the "M-G-M Fanfare" and collaborated with lyricist Gus Kahn on "Gone" for the film *Love on the Run* and in the following year "Who Wants Love" performed by Joan Crawford in *The Bride Wore Red* soundtrack. Billy Holiday's subsequent recording from *Bride* gave Father his first big hit. In 1938 Louis B. Mayer loaned my father to David O. Selznick (Mayer's son-in-law) for *The Young in Heart,* which earned Father his first two Oscar® nominations for Best Original Score and Best Song. When he returned to M.G.M. the romantic comedy *The Philadelphia Story* (1939) was waiting for him—and my birth was just around the corner. After the success of these films, it was back to work for Selznick, on Alfred Hitchcock's *Rebecca* (1940), an inspired and memorable score, and I think one of his best. In 1943 he moved to Warner Bros. beginning an association that lasted for the next twelve years. Kate Smith's recording of "Old Acquaintance" from the film of the same name was very popular during World War II. *Objective, Burma!* (1945) from this period features one of the many patriotic marches Father composed during his years with Warner Bros.

The third and most prolific period of my father's career began in 1949 when he became a free-lance composer working mostly at Paramount and 20th Century Fox Studios in addition to Warner Bros. His first two pictures with Paramount, *Sunset Boulevard* (1950) and *A Place in the Sun* (1951) brought him back-to-back Oscars, a record that was unbroken for half a century. Surprisingly, the iconic movie *Sunset Boulevard* (1950) was not well received at its first preview. The audience laughed at the "Conversing Corpses" that originally opened the film. Director Billy Wilder changed the beginning to a police car-chase down Sunset Boulevard and my father was able to edit his original opening composition to fit the new start of the film. That version is arranged for piano solo in this collection. Father composed the magnificent love theme "Tonight My Love" (lyrics by Jay Livingston and Ray Evans) for Elizabeth Taylor's character Angela Vickers in *A Place in the Sun*. Elizabeth Taylor loved it, but director George Stevens hated it! In an unusual turn of events, Paramount Pictures supported their composer over the objections of the film's director. Some consider this to be my father's most iconic love theme. Other beautiful themes from his work at Paramount include "Many Dreams Ago" from *Elephant Walk* for Elizabeth Taylor's character Ruth, and *My Geisha* (1961) for Shirley MacLaine's character Lucy. Father's colleague, the great Victor Young, recorded "Lisa," the love theme named for Grace Kelly's *Rear Window* character, to popular acclaim.

The tremendous variety of songs in this collection can only be attributed to my father's astonishing versatility as a composer. The *Song of Terezin* is comprised of eight songs in a completely different style to any of the other music found in this collection. Based on the poems and drawings of children in the Terezinstadt Concentration Camp near Prague, these songs were composed in 1965 and are scored for mezzo soprano soloist, mixed chorus, children's chorus and orchestra. While composing *The Song of Tererzin* Father sought inspiration at the Children's Zoo in Central Park in New York, a block from our home, where he would go every morning with coffee and note pad in hand.

When Father agreed to compose the score for *Sayonara* in 1957, the inclusion of Irving Berlin's song was required as part of the assignment. However, it was his own theme that was used for the ill-fated lovers, played by Red Buttons and Miyoshi Umeki, who incidentally won Oscars for Best Supporting Actor and Best Supporting Actress. The "Katsumi Love Theme" was subsequently an international success, and when our family traveled to Italy the following summer for *The Nun's Story*, we heard it everywhere we went. Mr. Berlin wrote to my father, "This note is to congratulate you for your brilliant job of scoring the picture. Also to tell you how pleased I am with the way you treated my song, 'Sayonara.' Apart from all this, I thought your own music for the picture was wonderful. Not alone in such good taste, but just right for the mood."

Although my father and writer/director Preston Sturges only worked together on three pictures at Universal in the mid-1930s, they remained friends. My parents often dined at his Players Club on Sunset Boulevard in Hollywood. They collaborated only once, on a tender ballad, "Love-Song," published here for the first time with the kind permission of Preston's son Tom Sturges. Father's 13-picture collaboration with producer Jerry Wald represented a high point of both of their careers, and resulted in arguably his most memorable song, "The Wonderful Seasons of Love" from 20th Century Fox's *Peyton Place* (1957) and its sequel *Return to Peyton Place*. Recorded by Rosemary Clooney, the song was a big hit and became even more widely known when it was used as the theme for the thrice-weekly television series and two additional television movies based on the characters from the original film. Other well-known songs from this period include "The Indian Fighter," "This is My Love," and "Devotion" from *The Blue Veil*. The song "I Do" from *Prince Valiant* is also from the mid-1950s, and represents the first of many collaborations with lyricist Paul Francis Webster. Webster and my father went on to produce "Beloved Infidel," "Rosanna" from *Hemingway's Adventures of a Young Man* (also for Jerry Wald films), "The Song of Ruth" and "Cimarron" during the 1960s. "The Wishing Star" from *Taras Bulba*, with lyrics by Mack David (who also wrote the lyrics for "Many Dreams Ago" from *Elephant Walk*), is one of my father's most enchanting melodies.

Father was no stranger to writing under the pressure of deadlines, but some deadlines were extreme. In 1960, shortly after it opened on Broadway, we went as a family to see Dore Schary's Tony® award-winning play *Sunrise at Campobello*, about President Franklin D. Roosevelt's struggle with polio. After the play, we went to dinner at a favorite restaurant, The Russian Tea Room. Dore Schary was also having dinner there that night. Father went over to his table

to congratulate him on the success of his play and said that if it were to become a motion picture, he would score it for free! Much to my father's surprise, Mr. Schary was at the Tea Room to celebrate having just sold the film rights to Warner Bros. and said he would love to have Father compose the score, but not for free. When it came time for production to begin, Mr. Schary called my father and apologetically asked if he could come to the studio the following Monday morning and play the "Roosevelt Theme" for him and director Vincent J. Donohue. Father agreed, but by the end of the week we still had not heard any music coming from his studio. Sunday night came around, and producer David Suskind had been granted the first live American television interview with Soviet President Nikita Khrushchev. Almost everyone in the country was watching the 90-minute show. My step-mother Lella anxiously reminded Father that he had to go to Warner Bros. the next morning to play the theme for Mr. Schary. Every time there was a commercial break during the show, Father would get up, go into his study and we could hear him playing the piano. This went on throughout the broadcast and when it was over he asked us to come into the studio so he could play us the "Roosevelt" theme.

Franz Waxman's composing career spanned thirty-seven years, six studios, 150 films and two continents. In addition to his remarkable ability to compose memorable themes, he was a fine arranger and pianist. His attention to detail, and the great care he took in creating just the right setting for each of his song themes shines through in this collection. The amazing orchestrators Arnold Freed and Patrick Russ, working from my father's original scores, caught the spirit of his music and added their inspirations and skill. I know Father would have been thrilled to see his work published—some of it for the first time—in this collection. I hope you will enjoy these songs as much as I do.

John Waxman

Acknowledgments: Thank you, Stephen Biagini, Tom Cavanuagh, Ned Comstock, Nicolette A. Dobrowolski, Arnold Freed, Paul Henning, Alan Lareau, Jeremy Lawrence, Stephen Massa, Tom Sturges, Suzie Weston, and Mark Carlstein (at Hal Leonard). Without the dedication and skill of Patrick Russ, the editor of this collection, this publication would not have been possible. The final note of appreciation must go to him.

For more information, please visit the official site celebrating the life and music of composer/conductor Franz Waxman, **www.franzwaxman.com** *and peruse the extensive Franz Waxman Papers at Syracuse University, New York,* **http://library.syr.edu/digital/guides/w/waxman_f.htm**

More songs by Franz Waxman—including **All Alone; The Bride of Frankenstein; The Garden; I Feel Like a Millionaire; The Mountains Beyond the Moon; This Could Only Be Paris;** *and* **Wide-Eyed Girls**—*are available at* **www.sheetmusicdirect.us**

Franz Waxman in a publicity photo, circa 1929.
Photo by Atelier Jacobi.

Franz Waxman conducting the Weintraub Syncopators from the piano, Berlin, Germany, 1933.
Photo by Atelier Jacobi.

Franz Waxman with Zasu Pitts, during rehearsals at Universal Studios for "Something in My Heart," from *The Affair of Susan*, 1935. Photographer unknown.

Franz Waxman on the set of *Rebecca,* 1940.
Photographer unknown.

Joan Crawford, who sang "Who Wants Love" on the soundtrack of *The Bride Wore Red*, photographed at the Warner Bros. Studios with Franz Waxman in 1947 during the composing of the score for her film *Possessed*. They are looking at a brochure for the first Los Angeles Music Festival (1947-1966). Photo by "Morgan."

Gene Kelly presents the Oscar for Best Original Score of 1950 to Franz Waxman for *Sunset Boulevard*.
Photographer unknown.

Alfred Newman party, October 21, 1952: (from l to r) Franz Waxman, Alfred Newman, Bernard Herrmann, Ken Darby, Vinton Vernon, Alex North and Hugo Friedhofer. Photo courtesy of the Alfred Newman Collection, USC Cinematic Arts Library.

Franz Waxman studying a score at his desk in the studio of his Los Angeles home, 1958. Photo by his son, John W. Waxman.

Franz Waxman conducting "The Wonderful Season of Love," the Main Title of *Return to Peyton Place,* on the 20th Century Fox recording stage, April 5, 1961. Standing behind Rosemary Clooney is the film's director (and Clooney's husband) Jose Ferrer. Photo Courtesy Twentieth Century Fox Photo Archive.

Franz Waxman was the first American conductor invited to conduct the major orchestras in Russia: Moscow, Leningrad and Kiev. In concert March 24, 1962 in the Leningrad Concert Hall (now St. Petersburg). Photo by Lella Waxman.

Franz Waxman, age 13, Dresden, Germany, 1920. Photographer unknown.

Franz Waxman rehearsing "The Little Mouse" with the Children's Chorus of the Cincinnati May Festival, for the premiere of *The Song of Terezin*, May 22, 1965. Photo by Helzer Gray.

CONTENTS

(Songs with asterisks are appearing in print for the first time)

8	The Adventures of Huckleberry Finn *	*The Adventures of Huckleberry Finn*
16	Alone in a Big City	
24	Beloved Infidel	*Beloved Infidel*
11	Cimarron	*Cimarron*
26	Count Your Blessings – Theme	*Count Your Blessings*
32	Devotion	*The Blue Veil*
34	The Girls of Montparnasse	*Das Mädel von Montparnasse*
29	Gone	*Love on the Run*
38	Head Over Heels	*Paprika*
42	I Do	*Prince Valiant*
44	Indian Fighter – Theme	*Indian Fighter*
46	Ireland *	*The Spirit of St. Louis*
48	Katsumi Love Theme	*Sayonara*
50	Kissy Kiss	*Gruß und Kuß – Veronika*
55	Life Is Really Swell	*Scampolo*
60	Lisa	*Rear Window*
62	The Little Mouse	*The Song of Terezin (song cycle)*
68	Love-Song *	
1	M-G-M Fanfare *	
70	Magic Voyage *	
74	Manderley Ball *	*Rebecca*
80	Many Dreams Ago	*Elephant Walk*
82	My Geisha – Main Title	*My Geisha*
84	The Nun's Story *	*The Nun's Story*

86	Objective, Burma! *	Objective, Burma!
77	Old Acquaintance	Old Acquaintance
88	Our Worries Are Over	La Crise Est Finie
98	A Penny's Worth of Lovin'	Scampolo
104	Theme from The Philadelphia Story *	The Philadelphia Story
93	Poverty Is Everywhere	Das Mädel von Montparnasse
106	Rosanna	Hemingway's Adventures of a Young Man
109	Say That You Love Me *	
112	Something in My Heart	The Affair of Susan
116	The Song of Ruth	The Story of Ruth
124	Song of the Empress	Ich und die Kaiserin
119	Spice It Up!	Paprika
128	Sunrise at Campobello *	Sunrise at Campobello
130	Sunset Boulevard *	Sunset Boulevard
134	This Is My Love	This Is My Love
136	Tonight My Love	A Place in the Sun
138	True Love Is Waiting	Das Kabinett des Dr. Larifari
142	We Just Know	La Crise Est Finie
146	When You Love	Paprika
151	Who Wants Love	The Bride Wore Red
154	The Wishing Star	Taras Bulba
156	The Wonderful Season of Love	Peyton Place
158	Young in Heart	Young in Heart

THE ADVENTURES OF HUCKLEBERRY FINN

from the 1939 MGM Picture THE ADVENTURES OF HUCKLEBERRY FINN

By FRANZ WAXMAN
Arranged by Patrick Russ

Allegro con brio (♩ = 80)

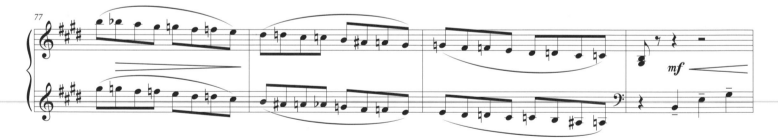

CIMARRON

from the 1960 MGM Picture CIMARRON

Music by FRANZ WAXMAN
Lyrics by PAUL FRANCIS WEBSTER

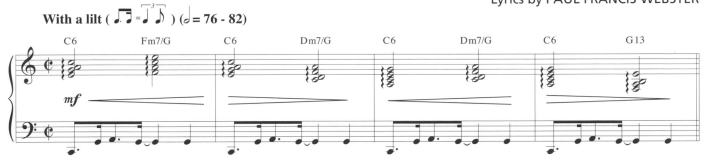

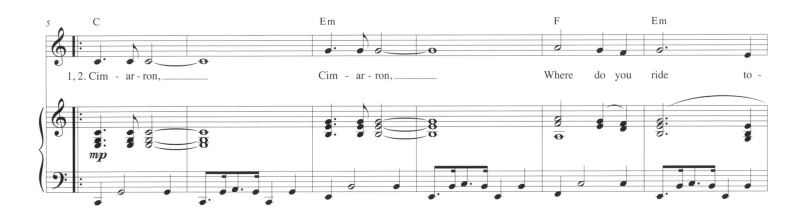

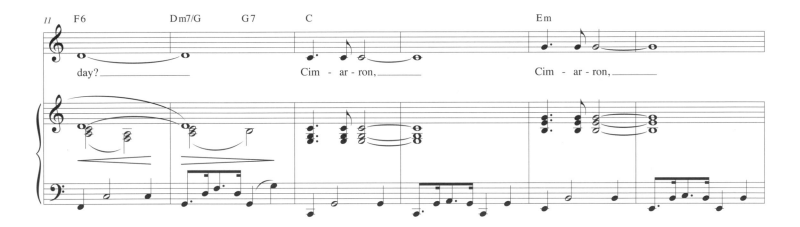

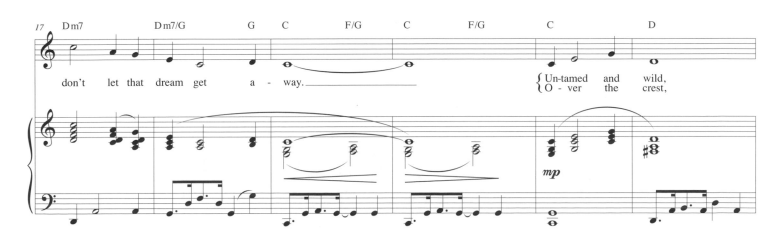

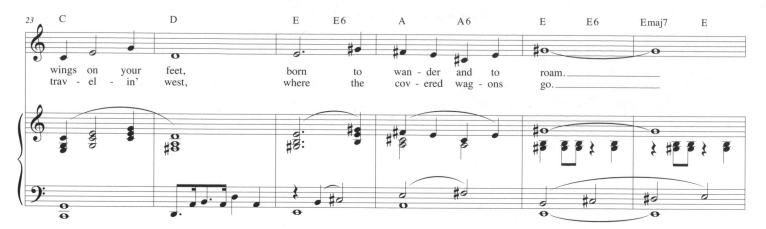

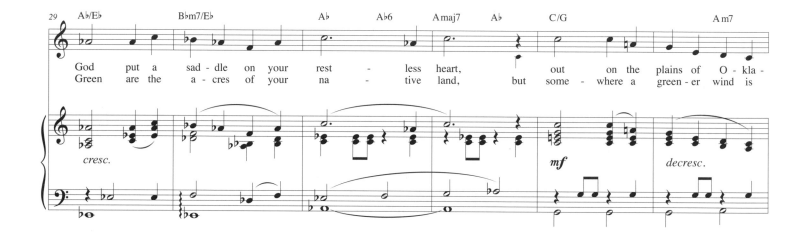

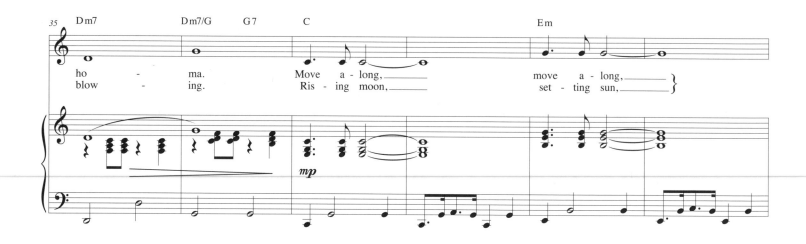

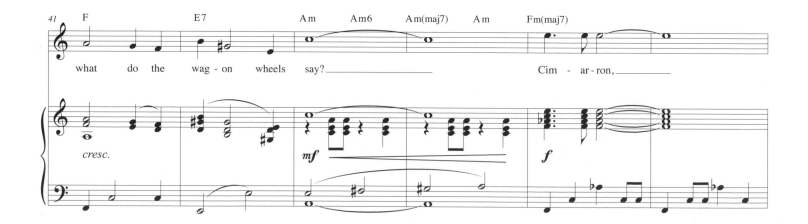

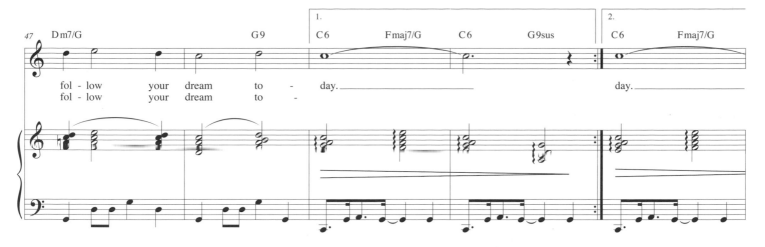

fol - low   your   dream   to - day.
fol - low   your   dream   to -   day.

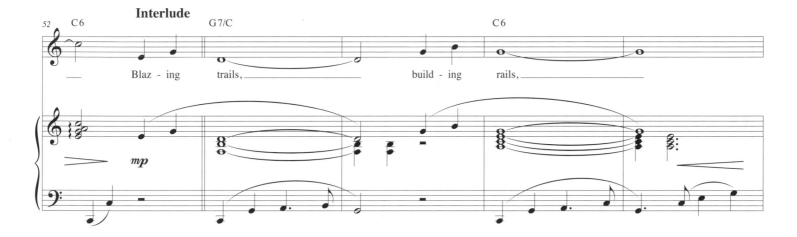

Interlude

Blaz - ing   trails,_____   build - ing   rails,_____

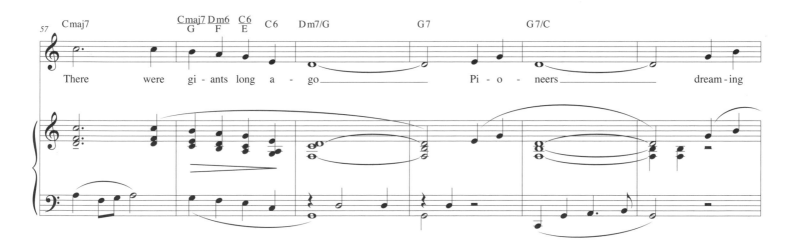

There   were   gi - ants   long   a - go_____   Pi - o - neers_____   dream - ing

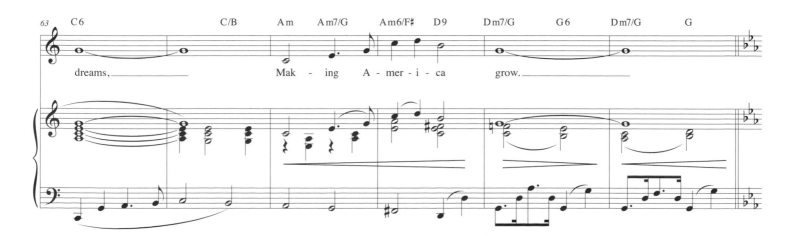

dreams,_____   Mak - ing   A - mer - i - ca   grow._____

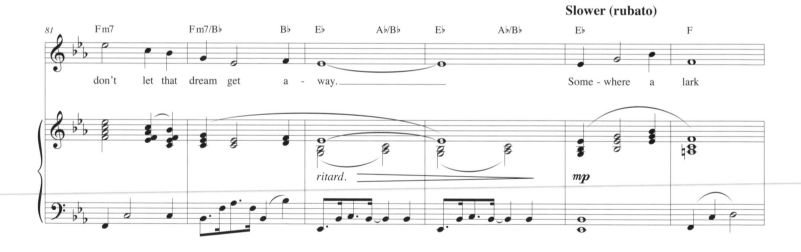

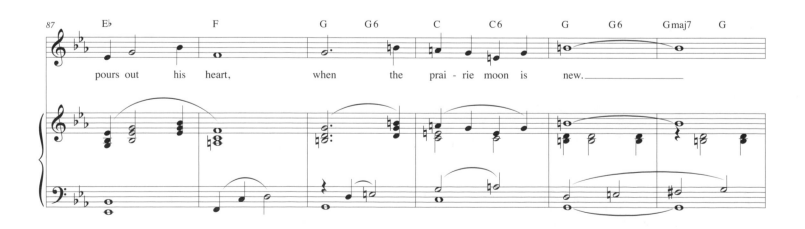

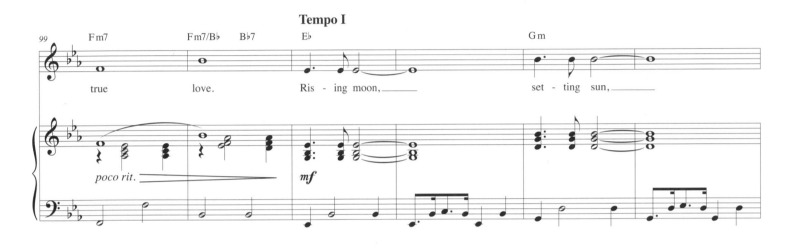

Tempo I

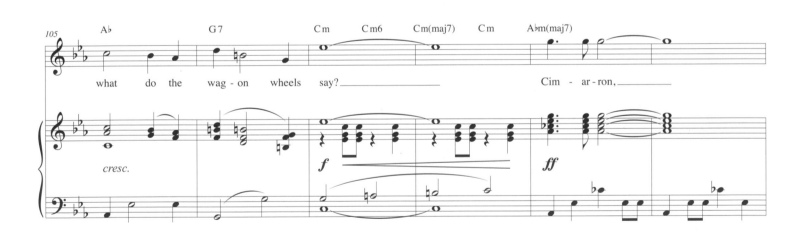

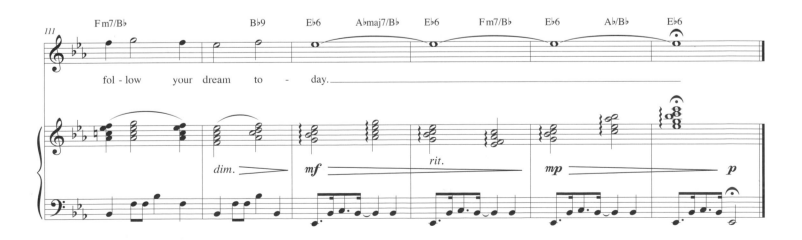

ALONE IN A BIG CITY
(Allein in einer großen Stadt)

Music by FRANZ WAXMAN
Original Lyrics by MAX COLPET
English Lyrics by JEREMY LAWRENCE
Arranged by Patrick Russ

1. Big cit - y life is fast and fun, Still you feel all a - lone,
1. *Man lebt in ei - ner gros - sen Stadt und ist doch so al - lein.*

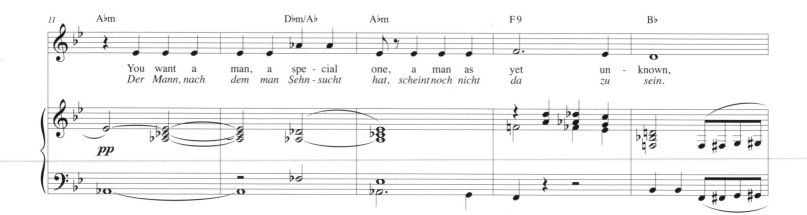

You want a man, a spe - cial one, a man as yet un - known,
Der Mann, nach dem man Sehn - sucht hat, scheint noch nicht da zu sein.

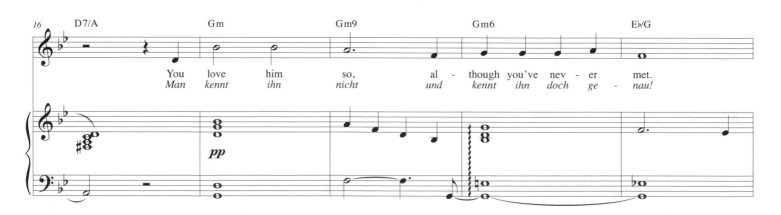

You love him so, al - though you've nev - er met.
Man kennt ihn so nicht und kennt ihn doch ge - nau!

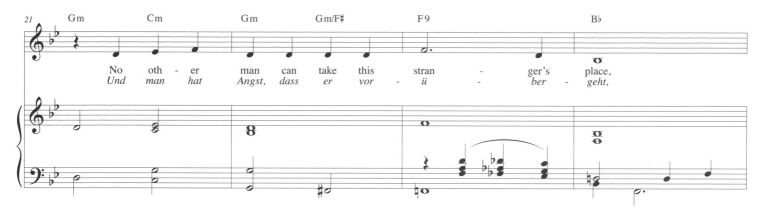

No oth- er man can take this stran - ger's place,
Und man hat Angst, dass er vor - ü - ber - geht,

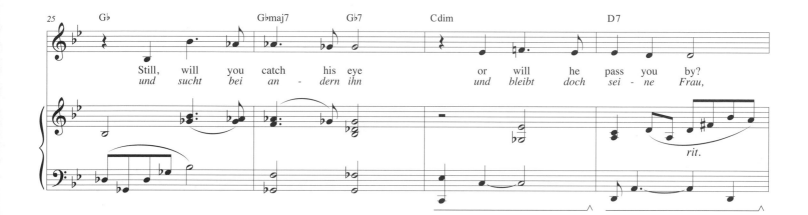

Still, will you catch his eye or will he pass you by?
und sucht bei an - dern ihn und bleibt doch sei - ne Frau,

rit.

Meno mosso (♩ = 40)

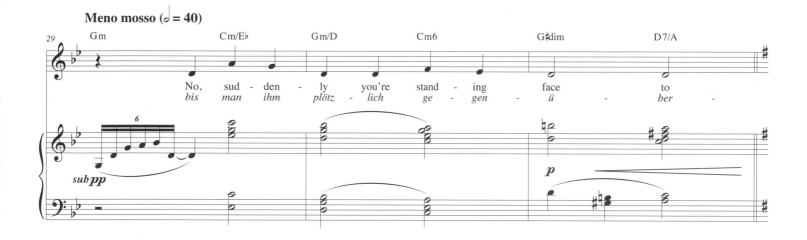

No, sud- den- ly you're stand- ing face to
bis man ihm plötz - lich ge - gen - ü - ber-

sub pp   *p*

In steady tempo (♩ = 52)

face.   And you try to speak, but the
steht!   Und da weiss man nicht, was man

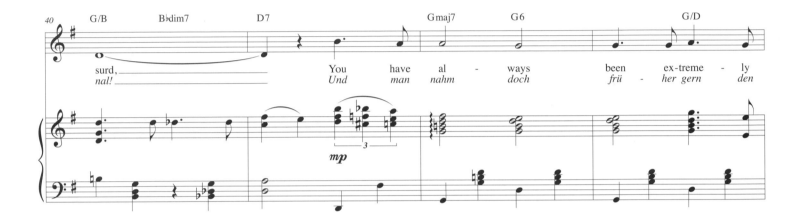

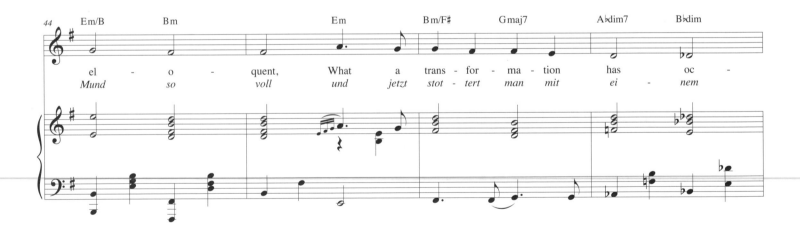

19

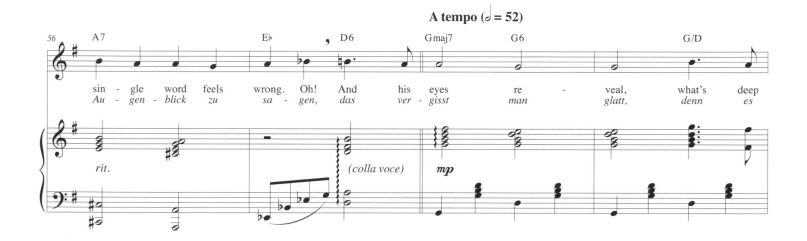

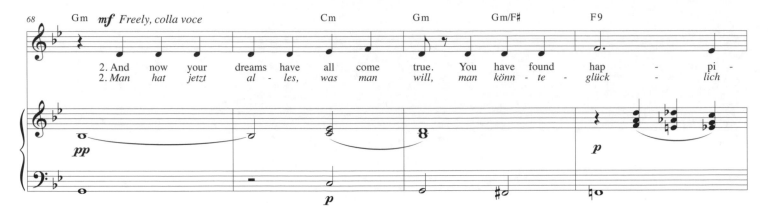

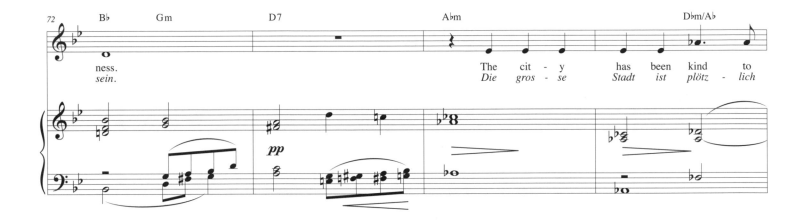

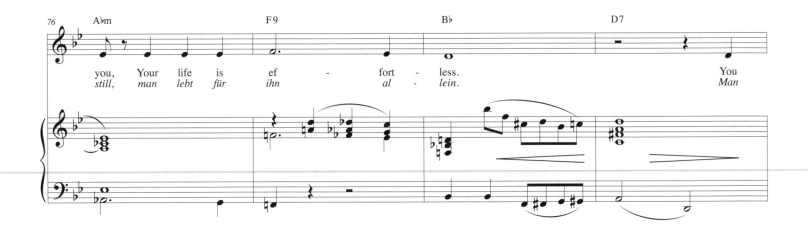

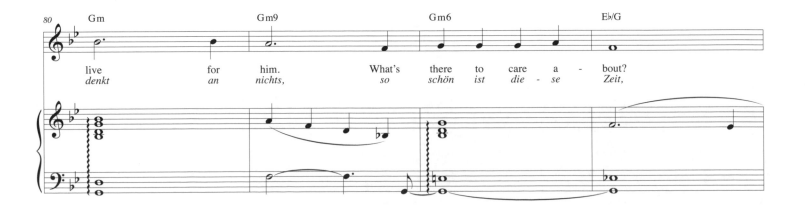

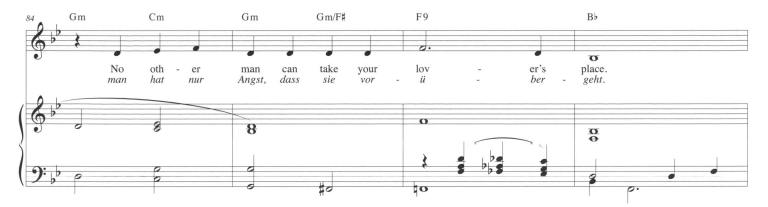

No oth - er man can take your lov - er's place.
man hat nur Angst, dass sie vor - ü - ber - geht.

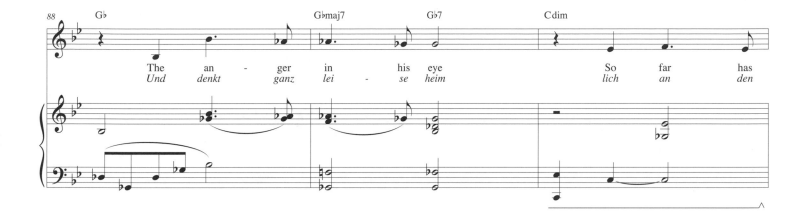

The an - ger in his eye So far has
Und denkt ganz lei - se heim lich an den

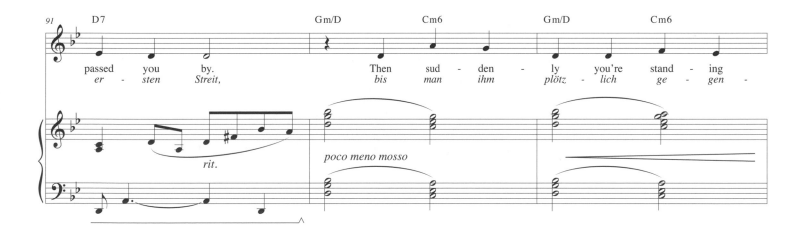

passed you by. Then sud - den - ly you're stand - ing
er - sten Streit, bis man ihm plötz - lich ge - gen-

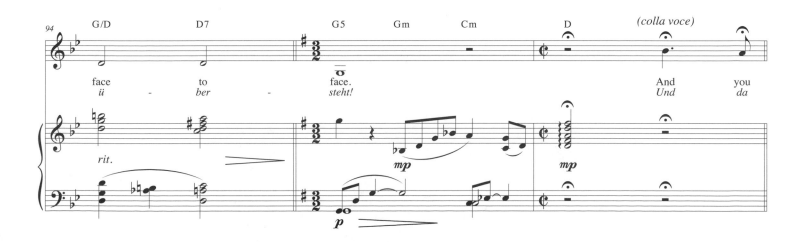

face to face. And you
ü - ber - steht! Und da

In steady tempo (♩ = 52)

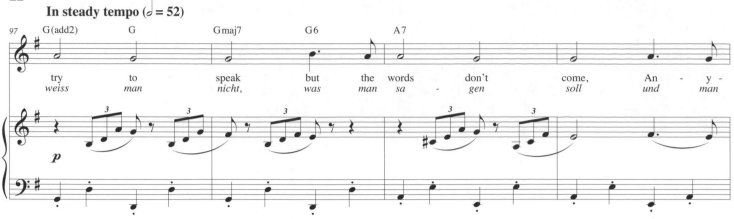

97

try to speak, but the words don't come, An-y-
weiss *man* *nicht,* *was* *man* *sa* - *gen* *soll* *Und* *man*

101

thing you'd say would sound ab - surd. _____ For your
fin - *det* *al* - *les* *so* *ba* - *nal!* *Und* *er*

105

qui - et man has start - ed scream - ing now. What a
nahm - *doch* *frü* - *her* *nie* *den* *Mund* *so* *voll* *und* *jetzt*

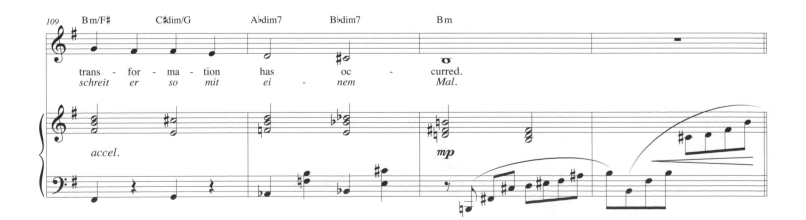

109

trans - for - ma - tion has oc - curred.
schreit *er* *so* *mit* *ei* - *nem* *Mal.*

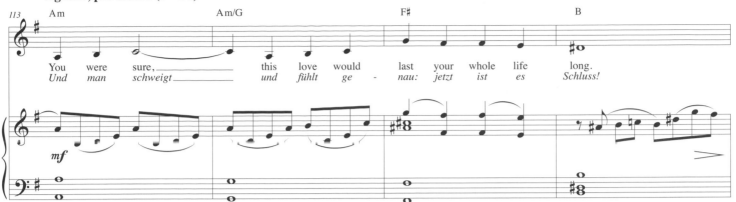

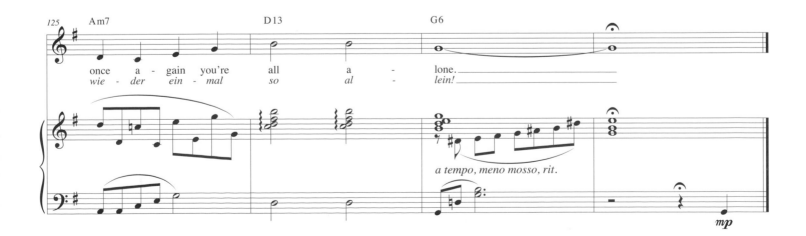

BELOVED INFIDEL

from the 1959 20th Century Fox Picture BELOVED INFIDEL

Music by FRANZ WAXMAN
Lyrics by PAUL FRANCIS WEBSTER

Moderately with expression

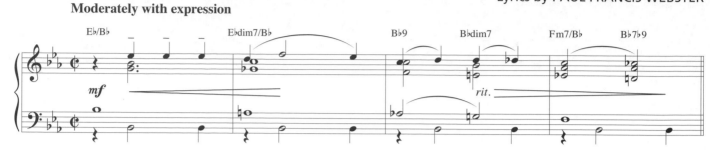

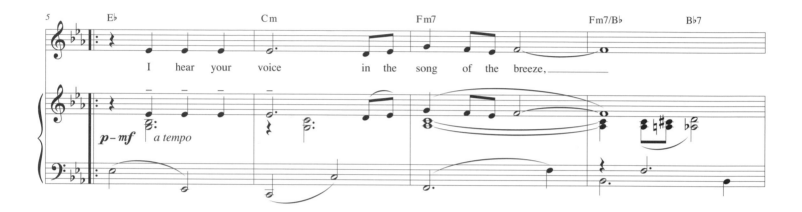

I hear your voice in the song of the breeze,

And I re - joice in the chance to re - prise;

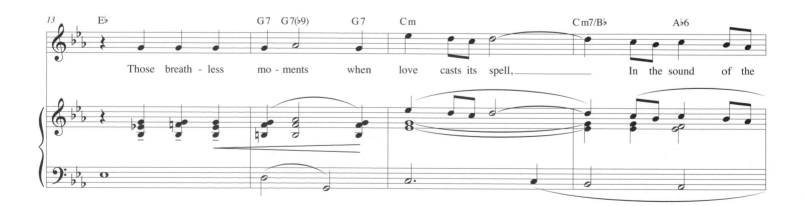

Those breath - less mo - ments when love casts its spell, In the sound of the

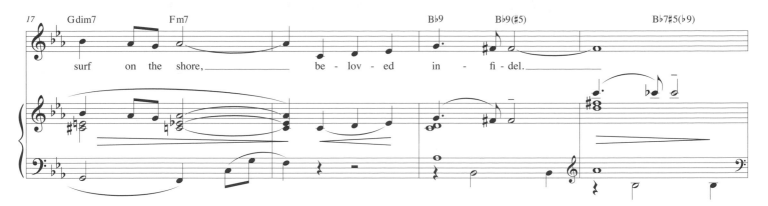

surf on the shore,_____ be - lov - ed in - fi - del._____

I see your face when I look at a star,_____ And I em -

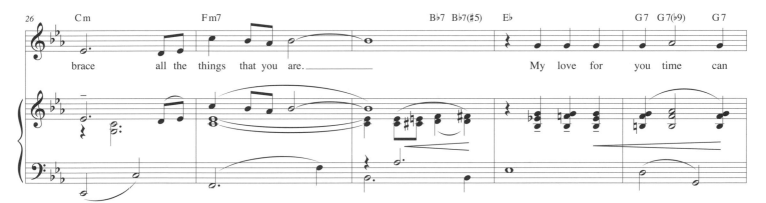

brace all the things that you are._____ My love for you time can

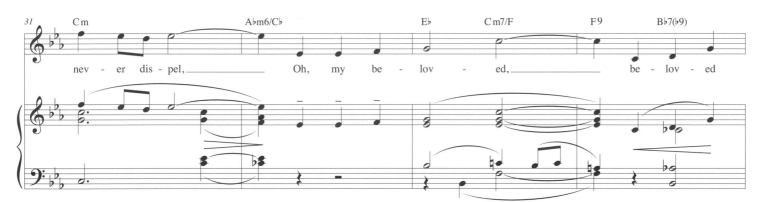

nev - er dis - pel,_____ Oh, my be - lov - ed,_____ be - lov - ed

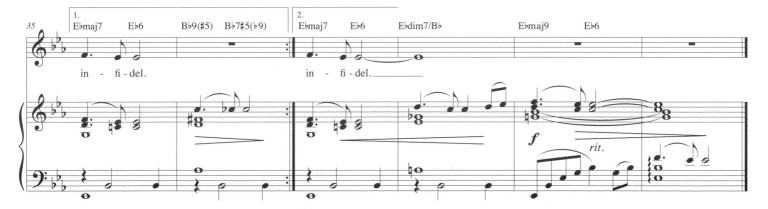

in - fi - del. in - fi - del._____

COUNT YOUR BLESSINGS – THEME

from the 1959 MGM Picture COUNT YOUR BLESSINGS

By FRANZ WAXMAN

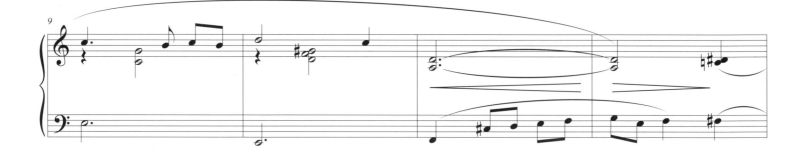

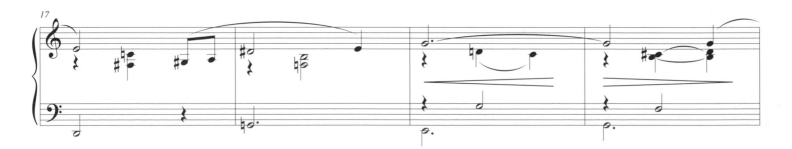

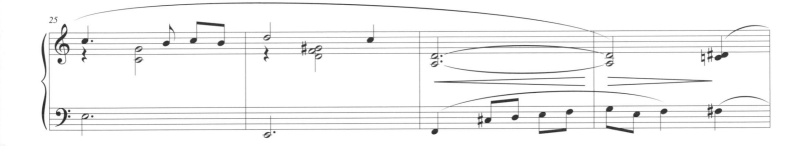

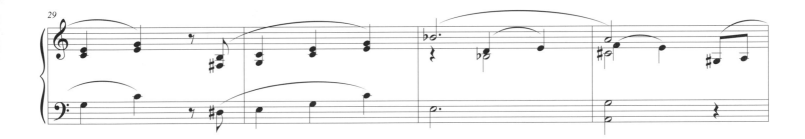

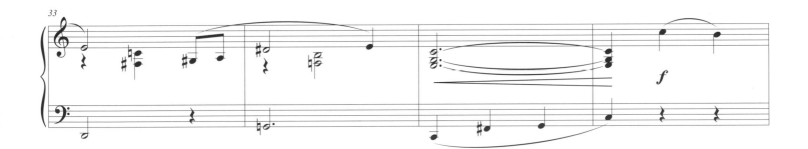

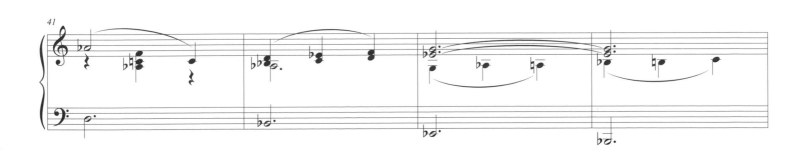

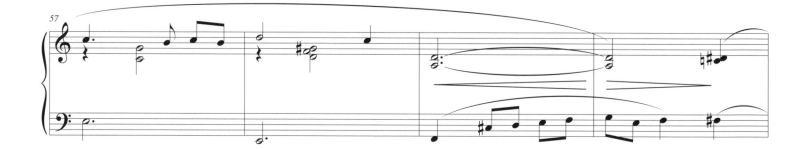

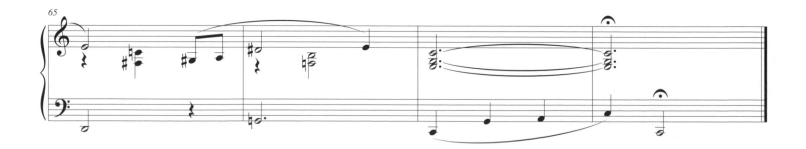

GONE

from the 1936 MGM Picture LOVE ON THE RUN

Music by FRANZ WAXMAN
Lyrics by GUS KAHN

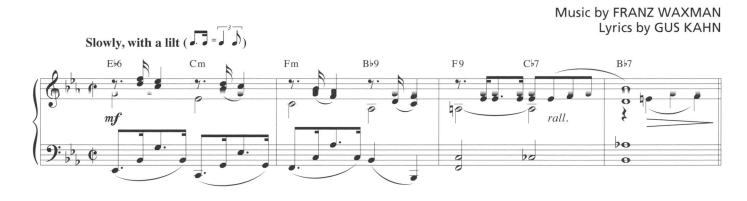

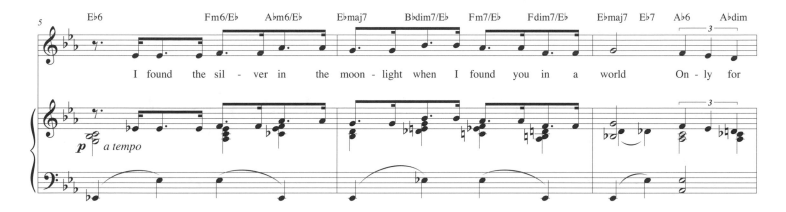

I found the sil - ver in the moon - light when I found you in a world On - ly for

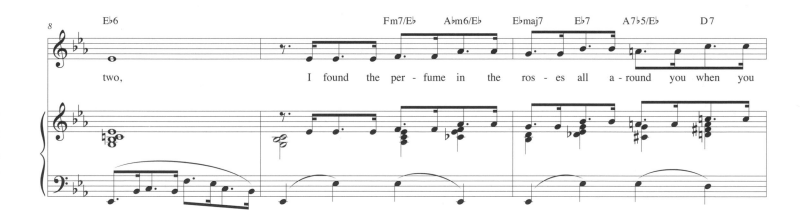

two, I found the per - fume in the ros - es all a - round you when you

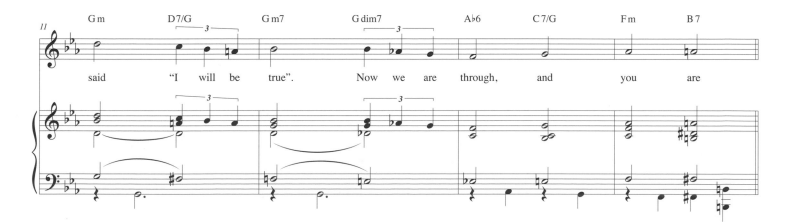

said "I will be true". Now we are through, and you are

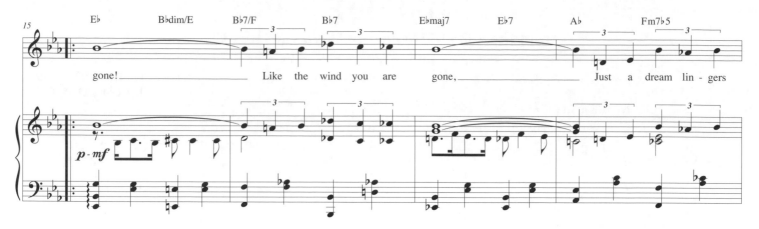

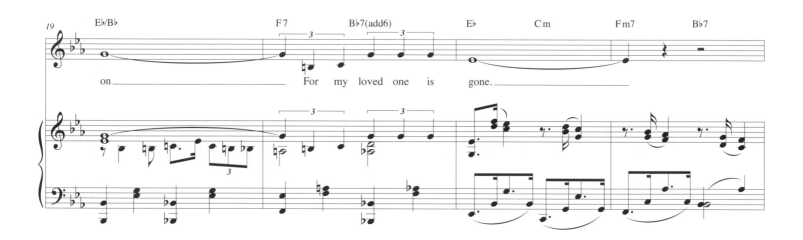

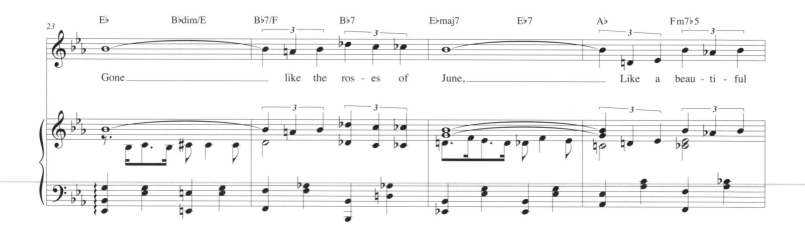

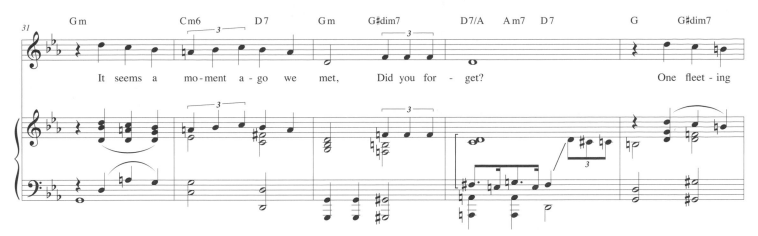

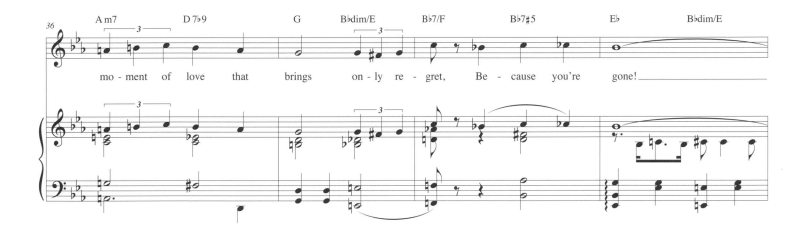

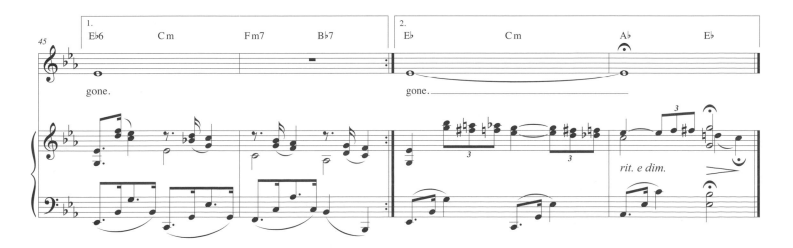

DEVOTION
from the 1951 RKO Radio Picture THE BLUE VEIL

Music by FRANZ WAXMAN
Lyrics by JACK BROOKS

Moderately slow and very expressively

Though the moon falls from a- bove, Though the tree may lose the dove, Still you'll

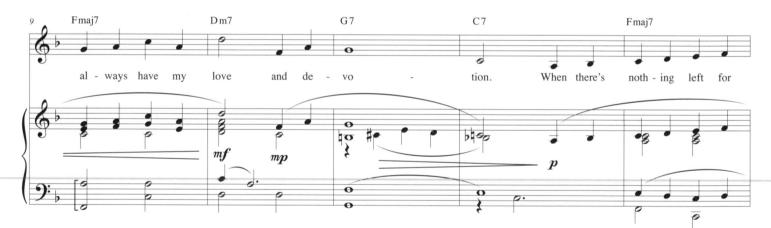

al - ways have my love and de - vo - tion. When there's noth-ing left for

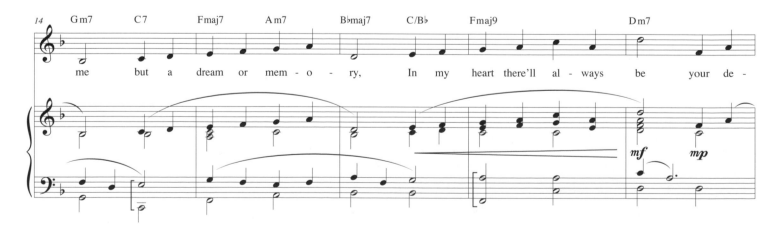

me but a dream or mem-o-ry, In my heart there'll al-ways be your de-

Slightly faster

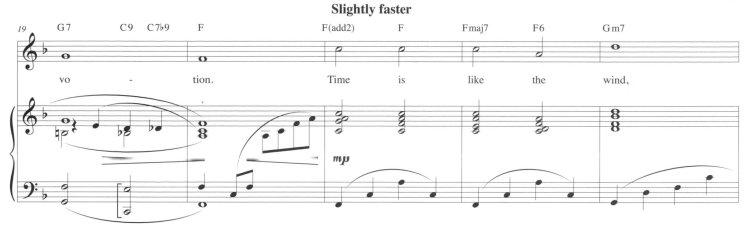

Time is like the wind, vo - tion.

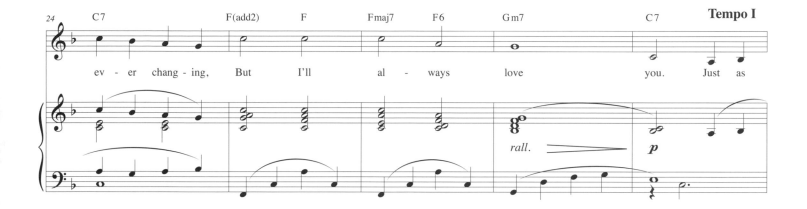

Tempo I

ev - er chang - ing, But I'll al - ways love you. Just as

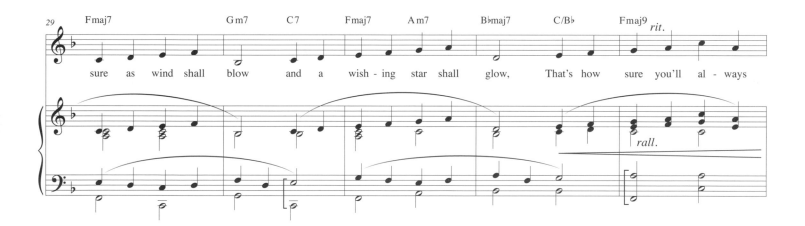

sure as wind shall blow and a wish - ing star shall glow, That's how sure you'll al - ways

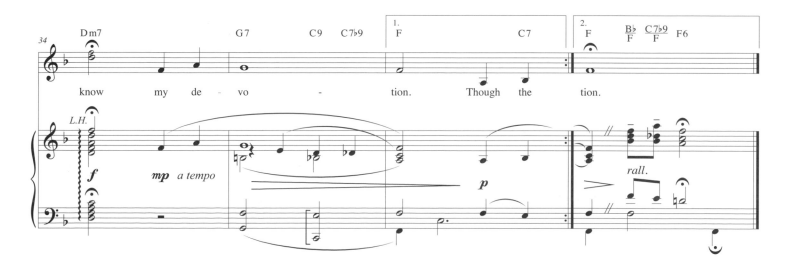

know my de - vo - tion. Though the tion.

THE GIRLS OF MONTPARNASSE
(Die Mädels von Montparnasse)
from the 1932 film DAS MÄDEL VON MONTPARNASSE

Music by FRANZ WAXMAN
Original Lyrics by ROBERT GILBERT
English Lyrics by JEREMY LAWRENCE
Arranged by Arnold Freed

Andante (quasi improvisso)

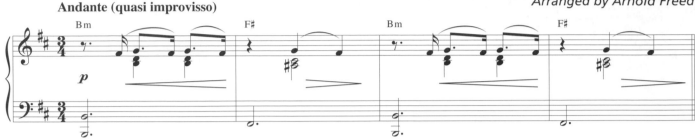

1. We have-n't an-y cav-i-ar, Nor do we have cham-pagne. Stone broke in fact is
2. *Wir ha-ben kei-nen Ka-vi-ar, wir ha-ben kei-nen Sekt! Uns fehlt der klei-ne*

what we are, With hun-ger on the brain. But when I touch your fin-ger tips,
Scheck in bar, der un-ser Tisch-lein deckt. Hab' we-der Geld noch Grund-be-sitz,

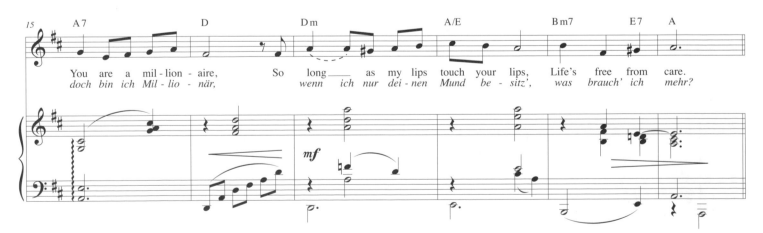

You are a mil-lion-aire, So long____ as my lips touch your lips, Life's free from care.
doch bin ich Mil-lio-när, wenn ich nur dei-nen Mund be-sitz', was brauch' ich mehr?

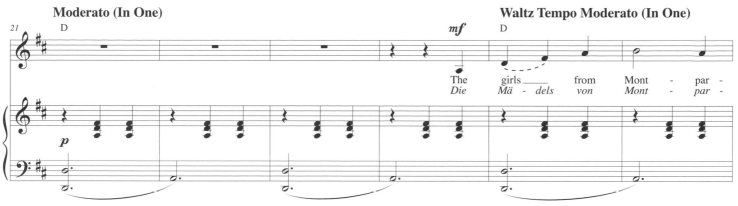

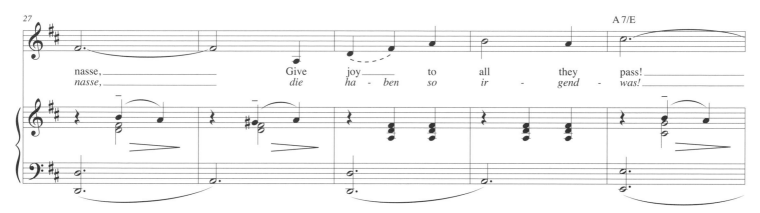

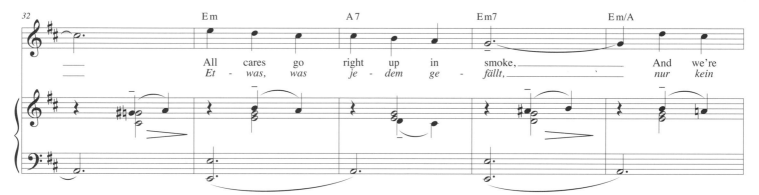

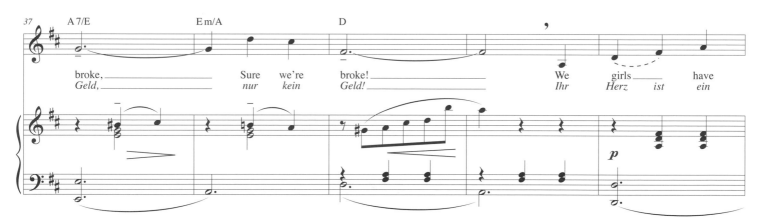

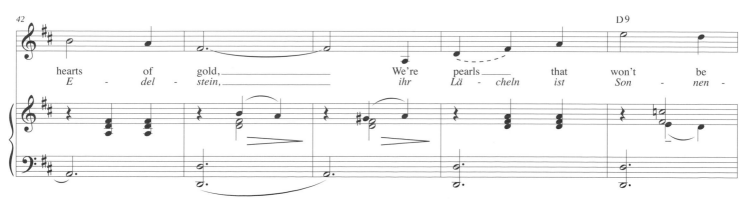

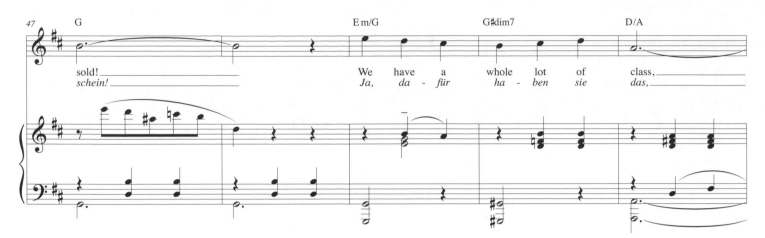

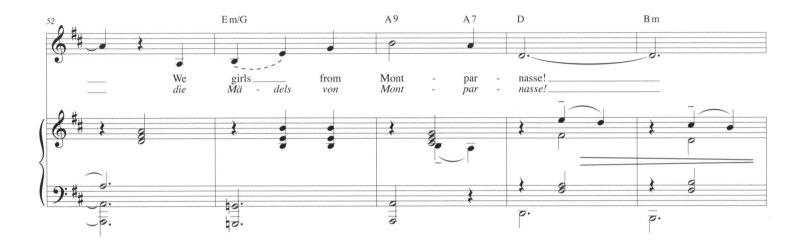

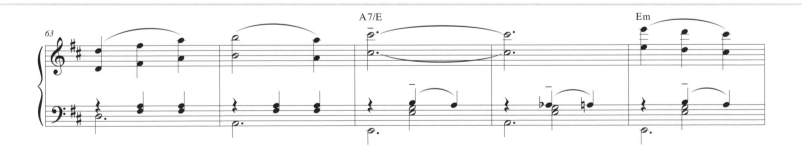

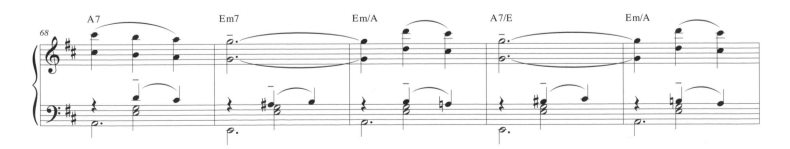

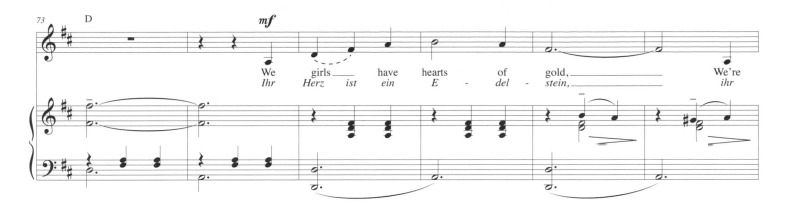

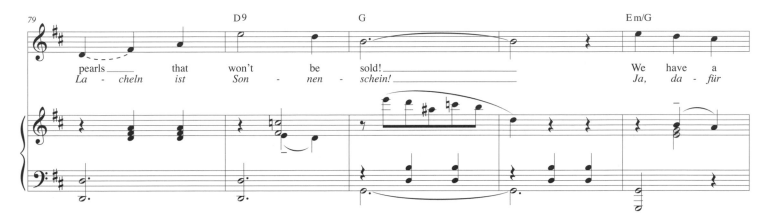

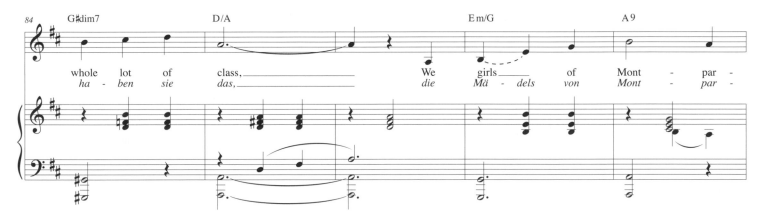

2. We specialize in happiness,
   We give it out en masse,
   And still we profit more or less,
   We girls from Montparnasse.
   One moment we feel hunger pains,
   Next moment they are gone,
   For whatever time remains,
   We'll party on!

2. *Jetzt woll'n wir alle lustig sein,*
   Mädels von Montparnasse,
   jetzt laden wir euch alle ein,
   hier ist für jeden was!
   Sonst saßen wir im Dalles da,
   meist war der Magen leer,
   heut' ist mal endlich alles da!
   Was wollt ihr mehr?

HEAD OVER HEELS
(Ach, wie oft kommt die Liebe unverhofft!)
from the 1932 film PAPRIKA

Music by FRANZ WAXMAN
Original Lyrics by KURT SCHWABACH
English Lyrics by JEREMY LAWRENCE
Arranged by Arnold Freed

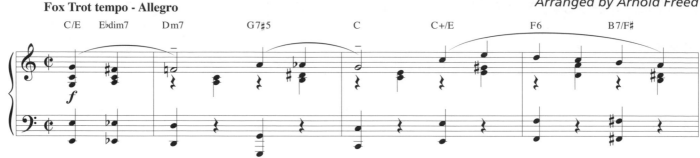

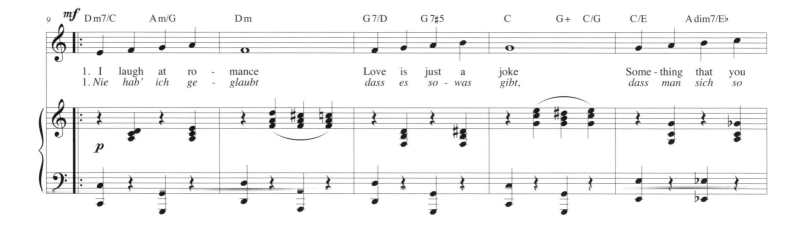

1. I laugh at ro - mance   Love is just a joke   Some - thing that you
1. *Nie hab' ich ge - glaubt   dass es so - was gibt,   dass man sich so*

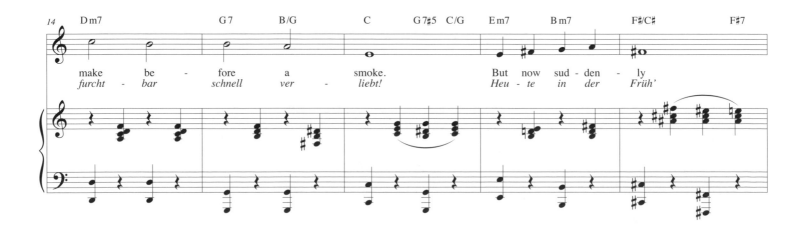

make be - fore a smoke.   But now sud - den - ly
furcht - bar schnell ver - liebt!   Heu - te in der Früh'

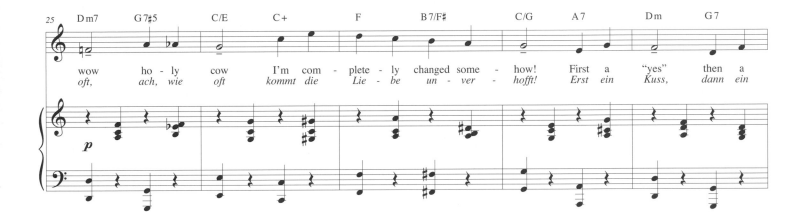

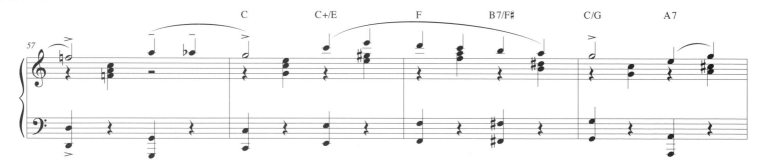

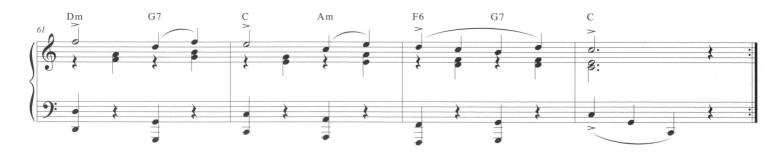

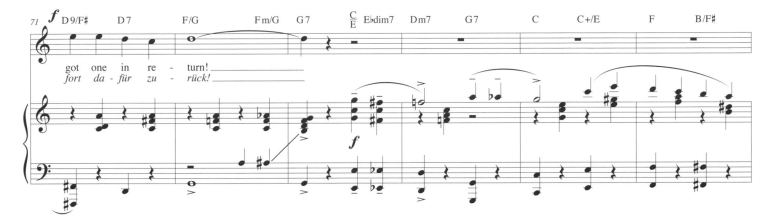

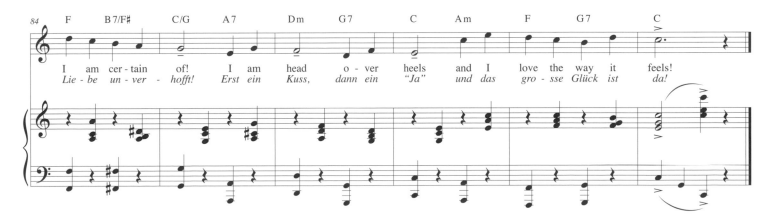

2. Analytic me couldn't analyze
How my strong resistance could capsize.
Sisters listen up it is not defeat
To give in to true love when you meet.
What I thought was so fraught ends up being quite sublime
It came fast but we'll last for a rather lengthy time.
Life ain't fair but a pair can square good times with the bad
And their love celebrates all the best times they both had.

2. *Für die klügste Frau kommt mal der Moment,*
Wo ihr dummes Herz in Liebe brennt.
Glaub' mir, lieber Schatz. Klingt es auch banal,
Irgend wo und wann trifft's jeden mal!
Ach, wie oft, ach, wie oft kommt die Liebe unverhofft!
Erst ein Kuss, dann ein "Ja" und das grosse Glück ist da!
Ach, wie oft, ach, wie oft kommt die Liebe unverhofft!
Eh' man's denkt, eh' man's denkt, hat man schon sein Herz verschenkt.

I DO

from the 1954 20th Century Fox Picture PRINCE VALIANT

Music by FRANZ WAXMAN
Lyrics by KENNETH DARBY

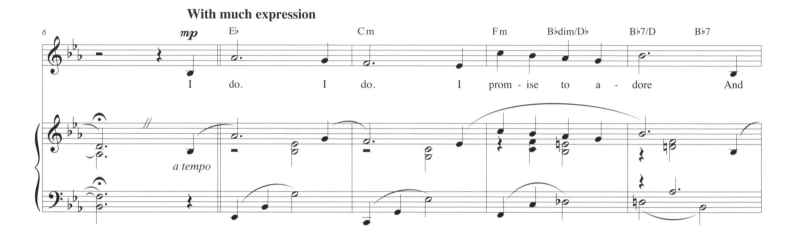

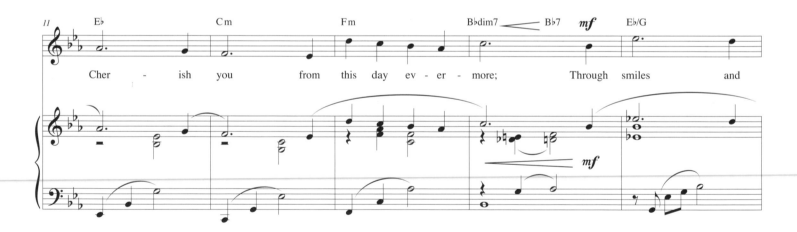

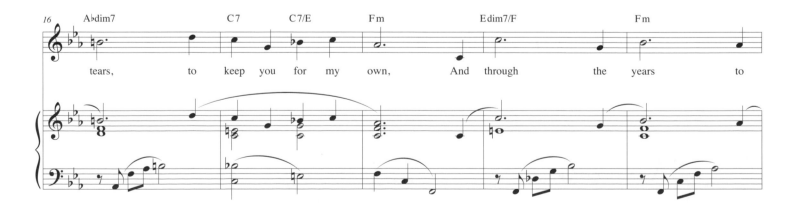

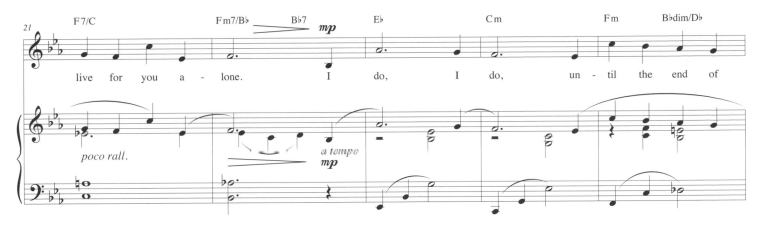

live for you a - lone. I do, I do, un - til the end of

time, I cling to you for heav - en made you mine, To

have and hold and make your dreams come true. With all my

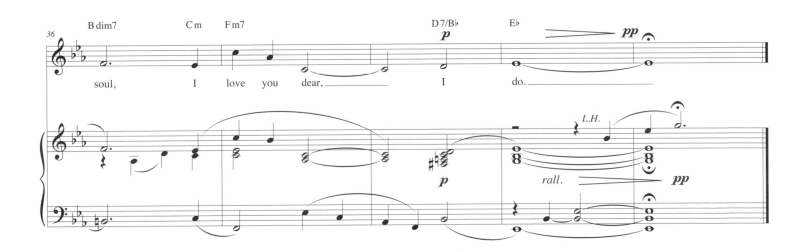

soul, I love you dear,_____ I do._____

INDIAN FIGHTER – THEME

from the 1956 United Artists Picture INDIAN FIGHTER

Music by FRANZ WAXMAN
Lyrics by IRVING GORDON

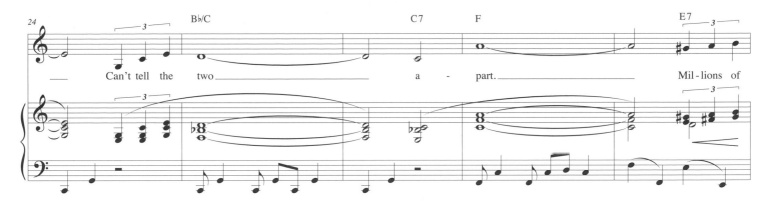

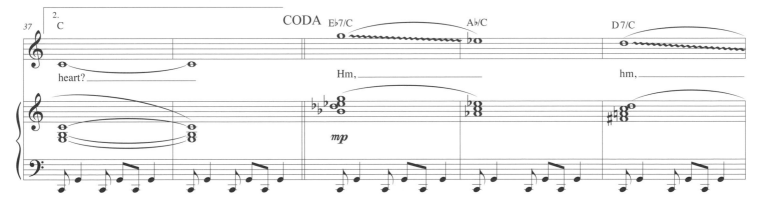

IRELAND
from the 1957 Warner Bros. Picture THE SPIRIT OF ST. LOUIS

By FRANZ WAXMAN
Arranged by Patrick Russ

Irish Jig (♩. = 132)

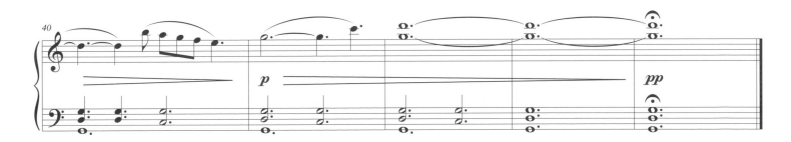

KATSUMI LOVE THEME
from the 1957 Warner Bros. Picture SAYONARA

By FRANZ WAXMAN

Broadly

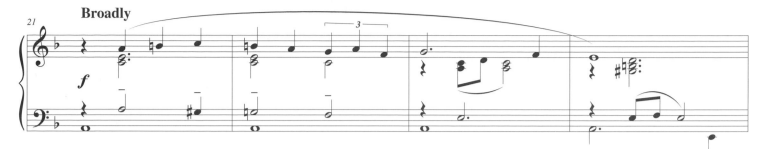

Tempo I

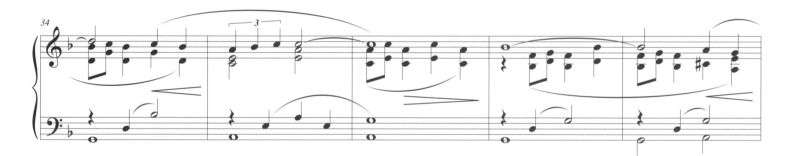

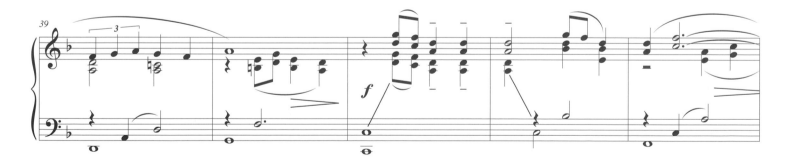

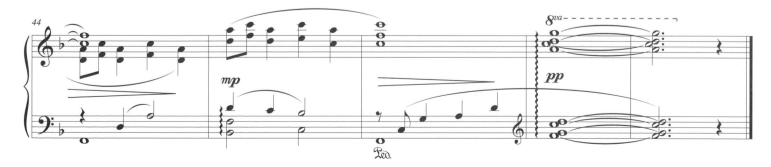

KISSY KISS
(Gruß und Kuß - Veronika)
from the 1933 film GRUß UND KUß – VERONIKA

Music by FRANZ WAXMAN
Original Lyrics by KURT SCHWABACH
English Lyrics by JEREMY LAWRENCE
Arranged by Arnold Freed

Fox-Trot Tempo (Lively)

1. When a
1. *Hat ein*

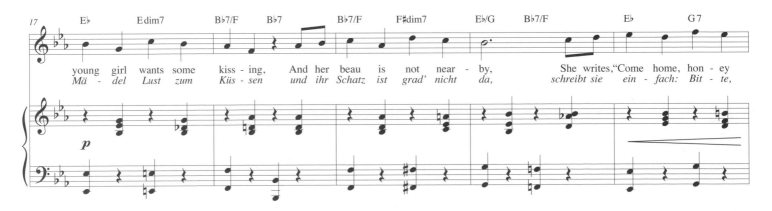

young girl wants some kiss-ing, And her beau is not near-by, She writes,"Come home, hon-ey
Mä- del Lust zum Küs- sen und ihr Schatz ist grad' nicht da, schreibt sie ein- fach: Bit- te,

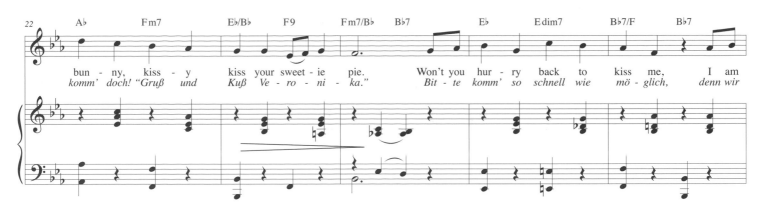

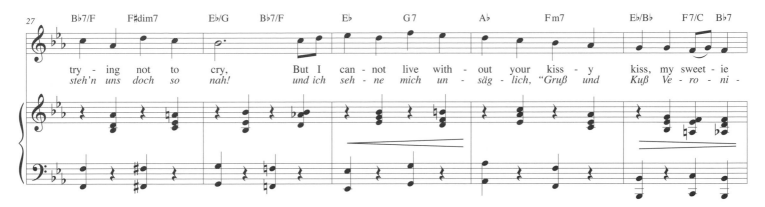

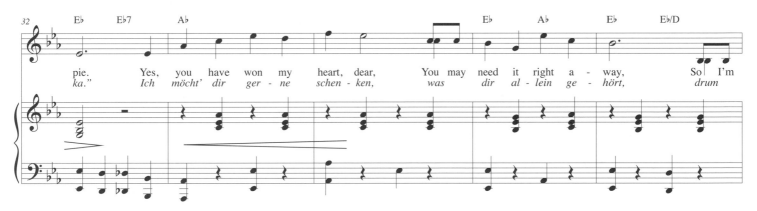

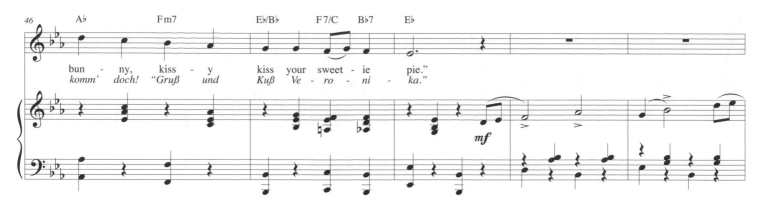

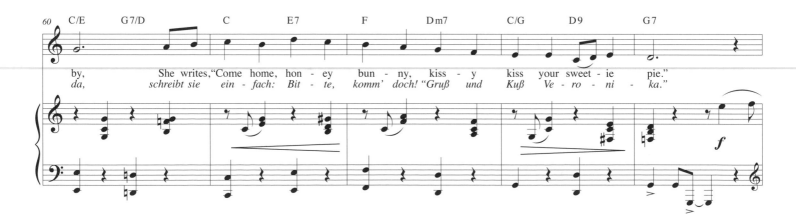

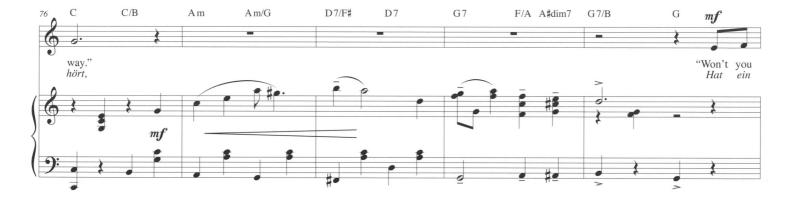

LIFE IS REALLY SWELL
(Ach, wie ist das Leben schön!)
from the 1932 film SCAMPOLO, A CHILD OF THE STREET

Music by FRANZ WAXMAN
Original Lyrics by MAX COLPET
English Lyrics by JEREMY LAWRENCE
Arranged by Arnold Freed

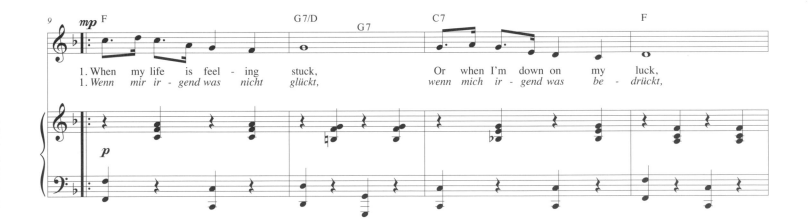

1. When my life is feel - ing stuck, Or when I'm down on my luck,
1. *Wenn mir ir - gend was nicht glückt, wenn mich ir - gend was be - drückt,*

I don't get de - pressed a bit, I won't be ob - sessed with it.
reg' ich mich nicht lan - ge auf, la - che nur und pfei - fe drauf.

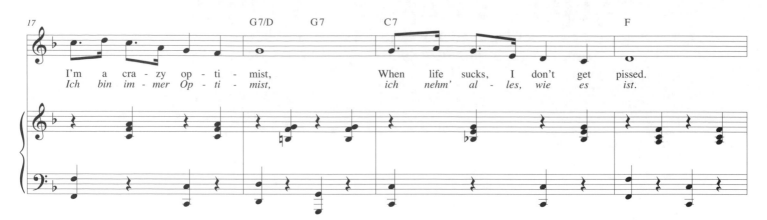

I'm a cra - zy op - ti - mist, When life sucks, I don't get pissed.
Ich bin im - mer Op - ti - mist, ich nehm' al - les, wie es ist.

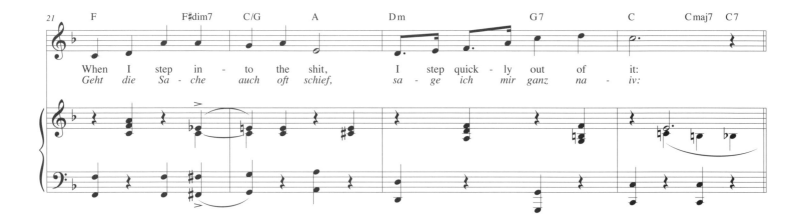

When I step in - to the shit, I step quick - ly out of it:
Geht die Sa - che auch oft schief, sa - ge ich mir ganz na - iv:

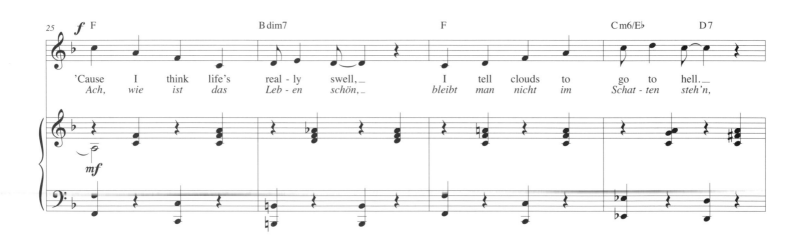

'Cause I think life's real - ly swell, __ I tell clouds to go to hell. __
Ach, wie ist das Leb - en schön, __ bleibt man nicht im Schat - ten steh'n,

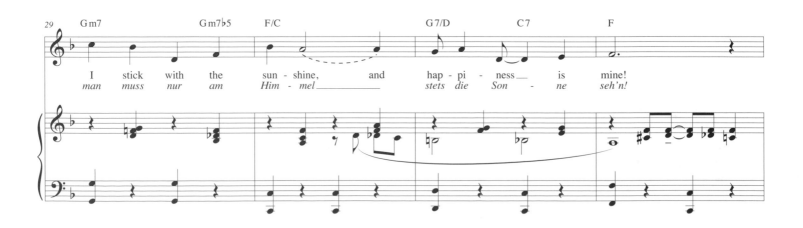

I stick with the sun - shine, and hap - pi - ness __ is mine!
man muss nur am Him - mel __ stets die Son - ne seh'n!

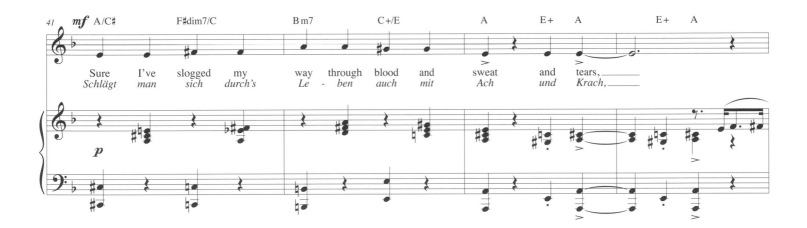

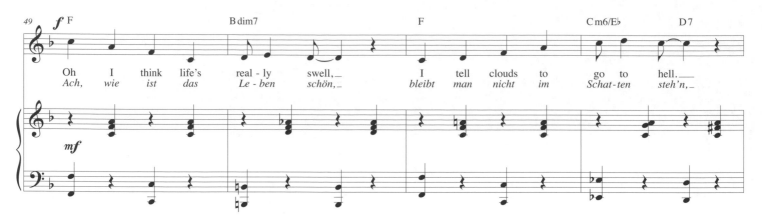

Oh I think life's real-ly swell,— I tell clouds to go to hell.—
Ach, wie ist das Le - ben schön,— bleibt man nicht im Schat-ten steh'n,—

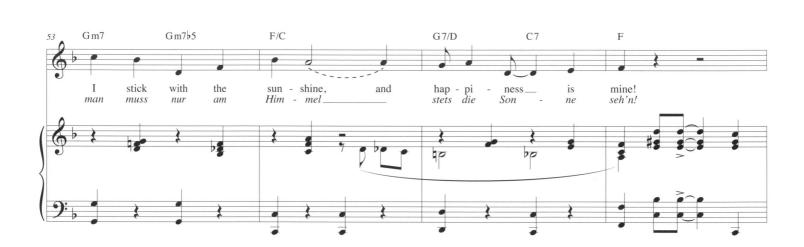

I stick with the sun - shine, and hap-pi - ness— is mine!
man muss nur am Him - mel_____ stets die Son - ne seh'n!

2. When you're sunning on a beach,
   Far away from worry's reach,
   Suddenly the rains come down,
   Soaked you almost swim to town.
   All bad thoughts you must resist,
   Always stay the optimist.
   Once home don't you start to cry,
   Just sing while you're getting dry:

2. *Wenn man einen Ausflug macht,*
   weil die Sonne scheint und lacht,
   und man liegt und sonnt sich bloß
   und auf einmal gießt es los
   und es schüttet so, dass man
   nur nach Hause schwimmen kann.
   Und im Bett als Optimist
   singt man, bis man trocken ist:

LISA
from the 1954 Paramount Picture REAR WINDOW

Music by FRANZ WAXMAN
Lyrics by HAROLD ROME

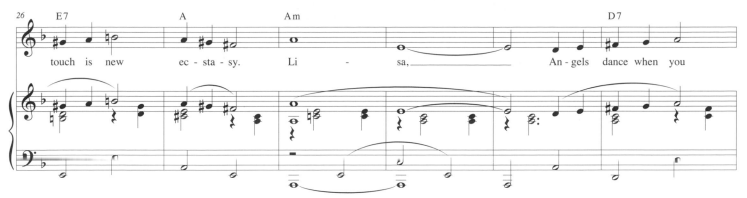

touch is new ec - sta - sy. Li - sa,_____ An - gels dance when you

cling to me._____ If this is dream - ing,_____ I

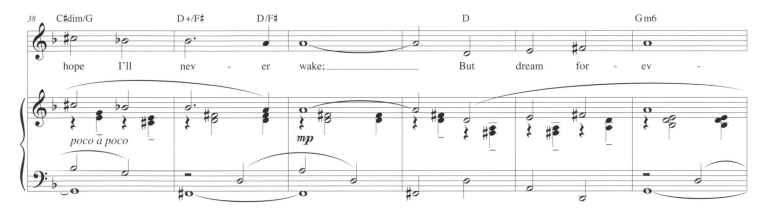

hope I'll nev - er wake;_____ But dream for - ev -

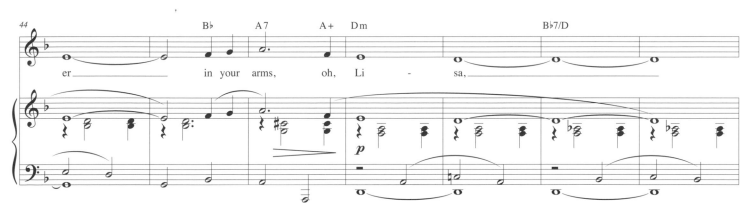

er_____ in your arms, oh, Li - sa,_____

Li - sa. Li - sa.

THE LITTLE MOUSE
(Das Mäuschen)
from the song cycle THE SONG OF TEREZIN

Lyrics by FRANTA BASS
English translation and Music by FRANZ WAXMAN
Arranged by Patrick Russ

Allegro frenetico (♩ = 126)

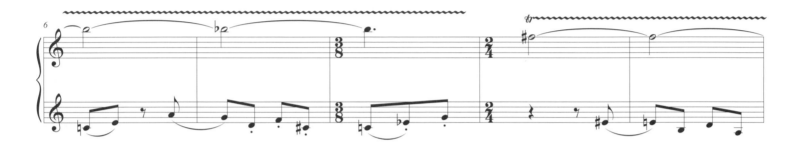

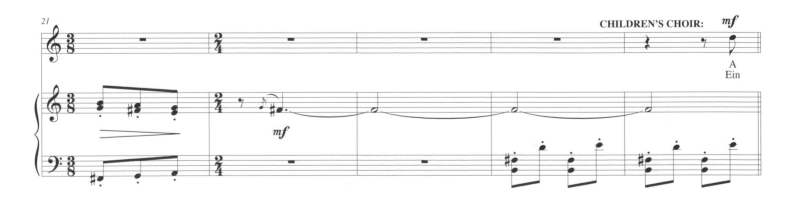

CHILDREN'S CHOIR:

A
Ein

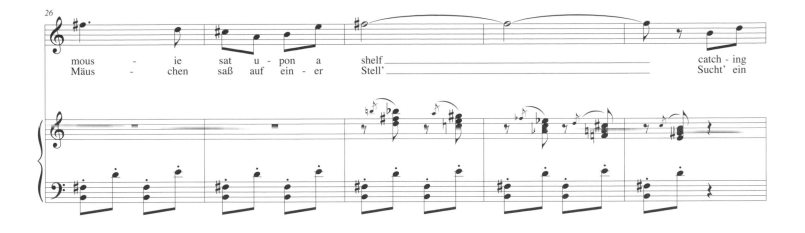

mous - ie   sat   u - pon   a   shelf _____ catch - ing
Mäus - chen   saß   auf   ein - er   Stell' _____ Sucht' ein

fleas   in   his   coat   of   fur.
Läus - chen   in   sei -   nem   Fell. _____

But   he   could - n't   catch   her.   What   cha - grin!
Doch   wie   sehr   es   such - te   es   nicht   fand

mf

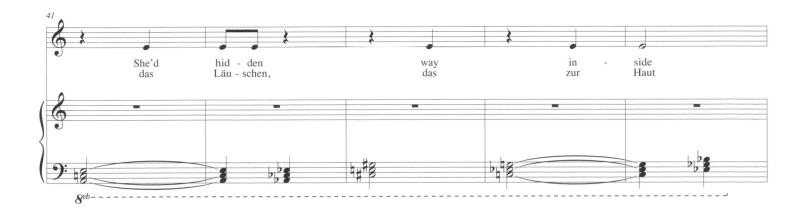

She'd   hid - den   way   in - side
das   Läu - schen,   das   zur   Haut

8vb- -

64

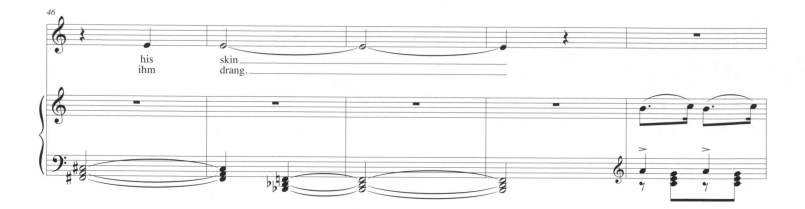

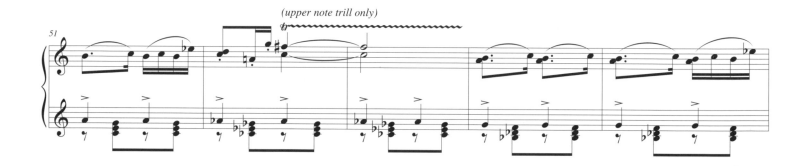

He turned and wrig - gled, wrig - gled, wrig - gled, wrig - gled, wrig - gled, wrig - gled,
es jagt im Krei - se, Krei - se, Krei - se, Krei - se, Krei - se, Krei - se,

He turned and wrig gled, wrig gled, wrig gled, wrig gled, wrig gled, wrig gled,
es jagt im Krei - se, Krei - se, Krei - se, Krei - se, Krei - se, Krei - se,

knew _____ no rest. _____ That flea was
hin _____ und her. _____ Die Laus dringt

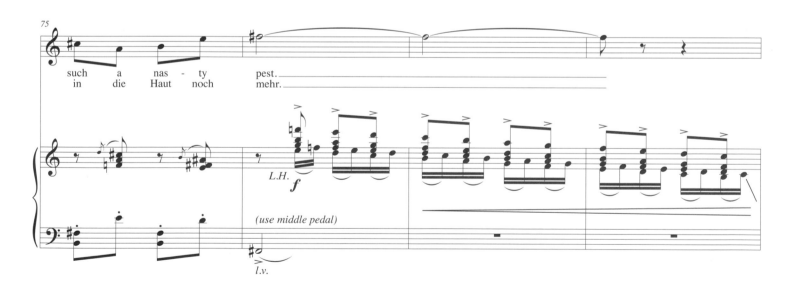

such a nas - ty pest. _____
in die Haut noch mehr. _____

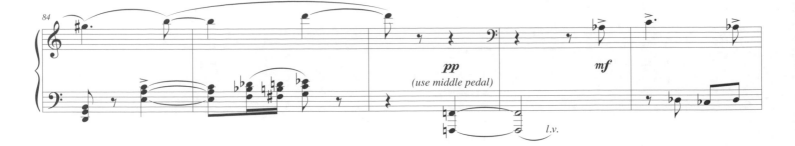

His Da - dy came and searched his coat,_____
Des Mäus - chens Va - ter kam dann schnell_____

_____ caught the flea and a way he ran_____ to
_____ und durch - sucht' ihm so - fort das Fell._____ Er

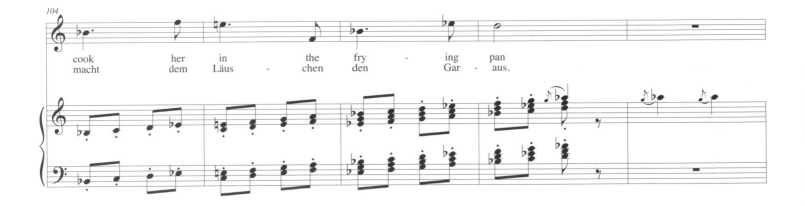

cook her in the fry - ing pan
macht dem Läus - chen den Gar - aus.

The lit - tle mouse cried _____
Und ganz be - glückt ruft _____

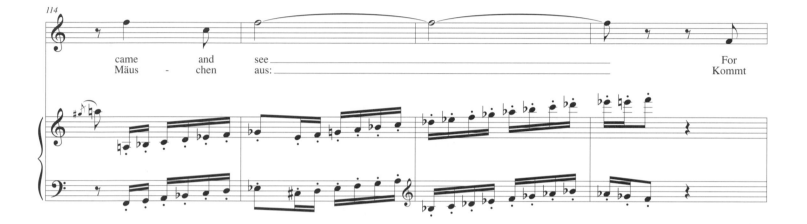

came and see _____ For
Mäus - chen aus: _____ Kommt

lunch we've got a nice fat flea! _____
al - le heut' zum Läus - chen - schmaus!

slap hands together
like a mousetrap

LOVE-SONG

Music by FRANZ WAXMAN
Lyrics by PRESTON STURGES

Waltz tempo (slow)

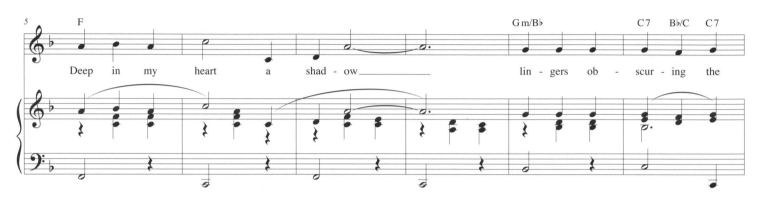

Deep in my heart a shad - ow _____ lin - gers ob - scur - ing the

sky _____ Deep in my heart there's an ech - o _____ Just the

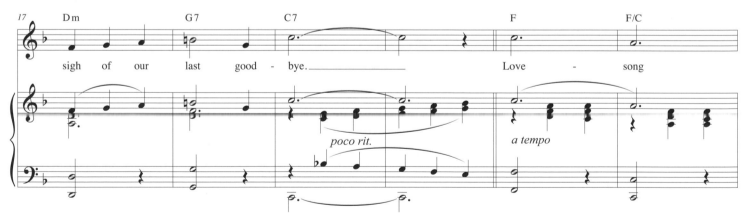

sigh of our last good - bye. _____ Love - song

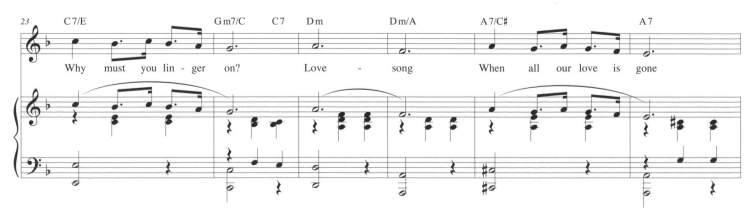

Why must you lin - ger on? Love - song When all our love is gone

Waking Aching memories Haunting Taunting

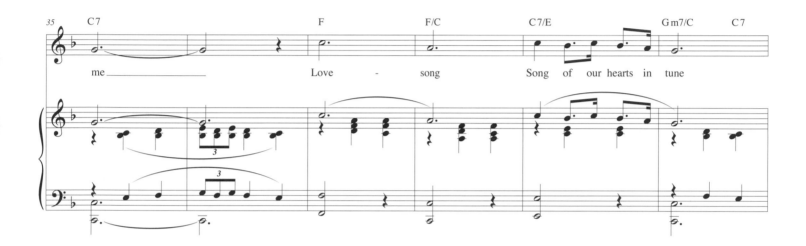

me___ Love - song Song of our hearts in tune

Love - song Song that we sang too soon Love - song

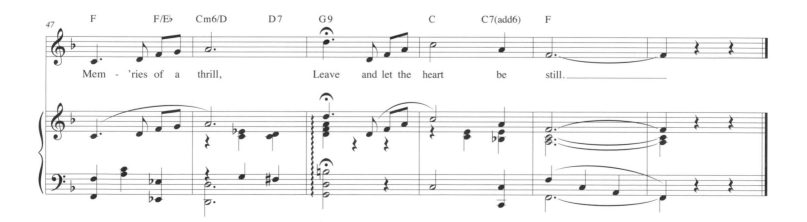

Mem - 'ries of a thrill, Leave and let the heart be still.___

MAGIC VOYAGE
(La Belle Croisière)

Music by FRANZ WAXMAN
Original Lyrics by LOUIS POTERAT
English Lyrics by JEREMY LAWRENCE

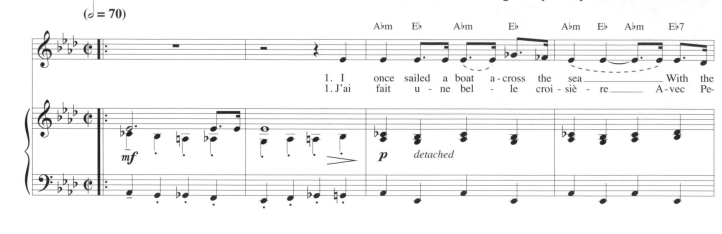

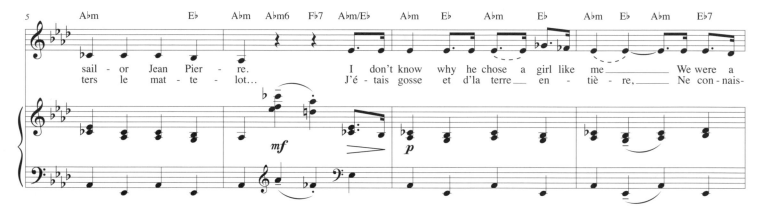

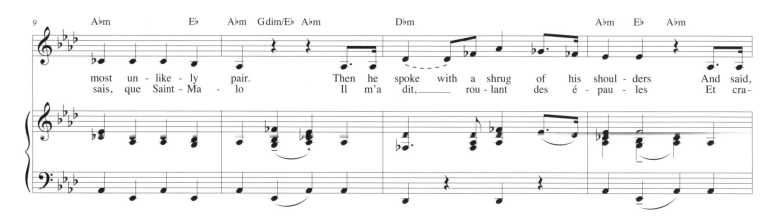

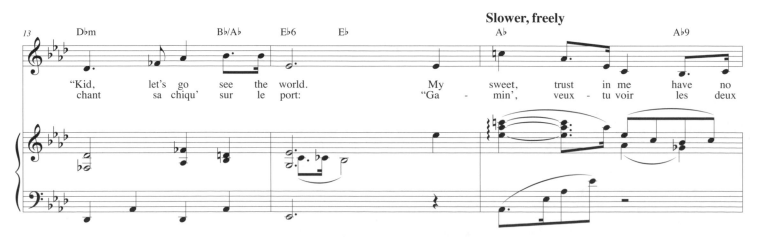

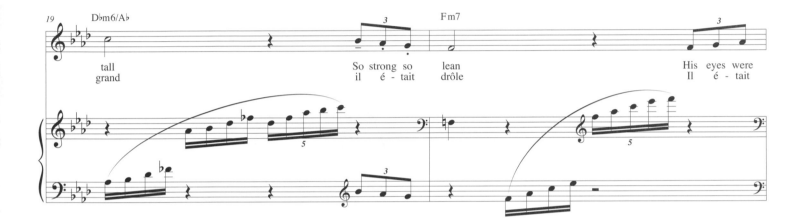

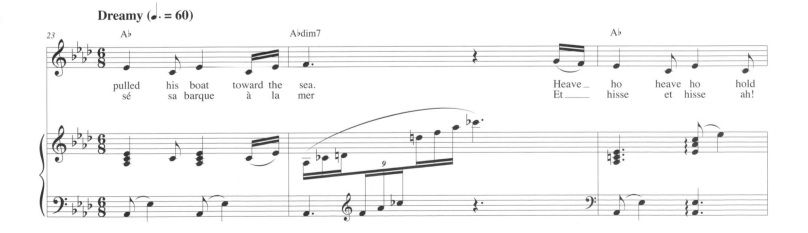

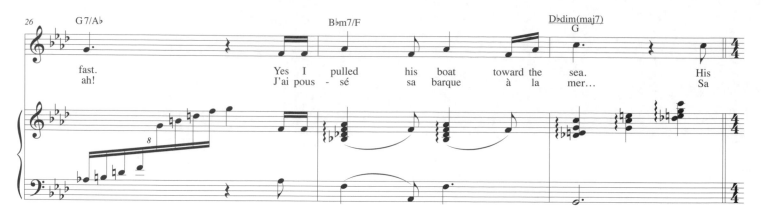

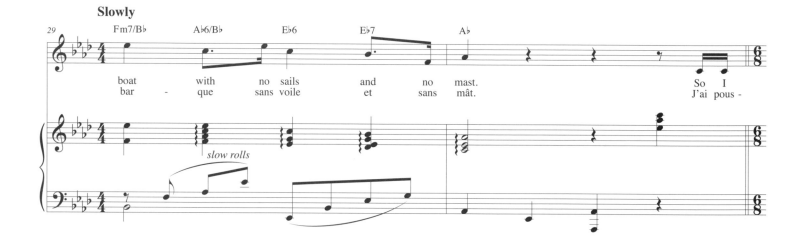

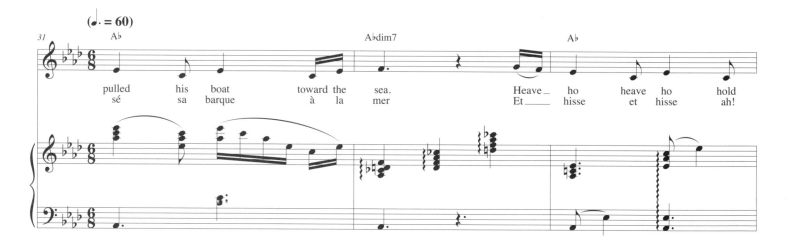

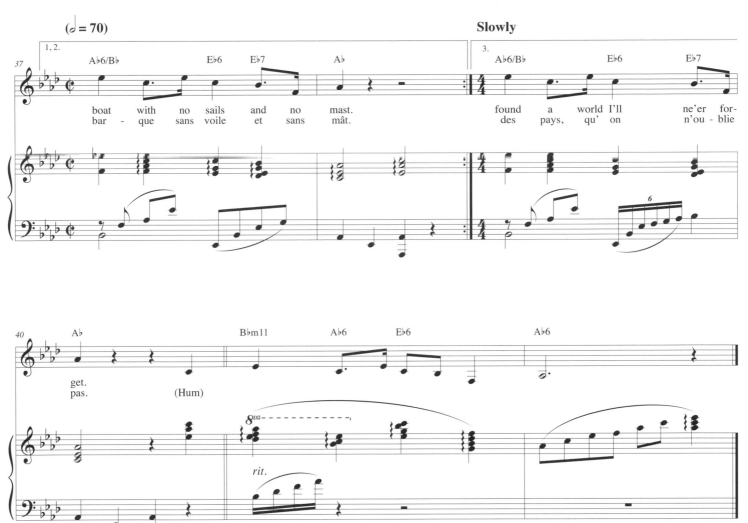

2. He thrust heavy oars into my hands
   And I took them willingly.
   We were sailing off to foreign lands.
   "Be brave," he cried, "row fearlessly."
   Suddenly his eyes started glowing
   When I looked through them, I could see
   Strange sights making me amazed.
   My eyes grew wide. My heart beat fast.
   Castles that seemed to float on air.
   Fountains of jewels beyond compare.
   So we sailed alone he and I
   In the magic of this place.
   He and I alone 'neath the sky
   Me wrapped in his loving embrace.

3. Once home I recited my story,
   But ev'ryone just laughed at me.
   Well no one likes another person's glory,
   That's what Pierre explained to me.
   In two hours, we'd sailed for forever.
   Two miles out, saw sights no one's seen.
   On my voyage with Jean Pierre
   As a young girl of seventeen.
   He was a man with magic eyes.
   A memory, I'll always prize.
   I once sailed his boat to a dream.
   Although my sailor's gone,
   I can still set sail on the sea.
   My voyage is still going on.

2. *Il mît entre mes mains dociles*
   Deux énormes avirons,
   Et m'a dit 'Rame' et m'a dit 'File'
   Courage, enfant, nous arrivons!
   Alors, j'ai vu, comme un mirage,
   Dans les yeux de Peters joyeux,
   Passer en d'étranges images
   Mille pays, tous fabuleux
   Et des palais faits de nuages
   Et des volcans d'embrun fumeux…
   Tout' seule avec lui sur la mer
   Et hisse et hisse ah! ah!
   Tout' seule avec lui sur la mer…
   Avec lui, qui m'a prise dans ses bras.

3. *Quand j'ai conté mon aventure,*
   Les gars du port ont ri de moi…
   Mais Peters m'a dit: Je t'assure,
   Qu'ils en ont vu bien moins que toi…
   En deux heur's de barque légère,
   A deux cents yards de Saint-Malo,
   J'ai fait ma plus belle croisière
   Avec Peters le matelot…
   Son torse est beau, sa mine est fière,
   Ses yeux sont doux, ses bras sont chauds…
   J'ai conduit sa barque à la mer
   Et hisse et hisse ah! ah!
   J'ai conduit sa barque à la mer…
   Vers des pays, qu'on n'oublie pas.

MANDERLEY BALL
from the 1940 United Artists Picture REBECCA

By FRANZ WAXMAN
Arranged by Lior Rosner

Tempo di Valse (♩ = 120)

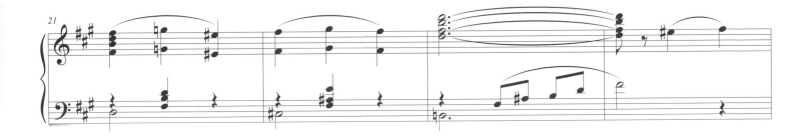

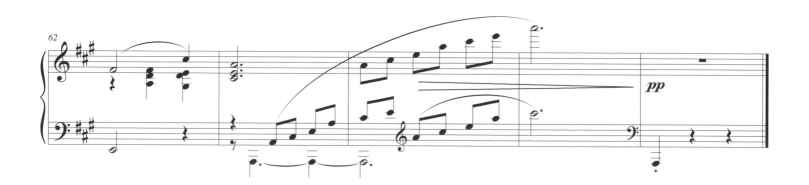

OLD ACQUAINTANCE

from the 1943 Warner Bros. Picture OLD ACQUAINTANCE

Music by FRANZ WAXMAN
Lyrics by KIM GANNON

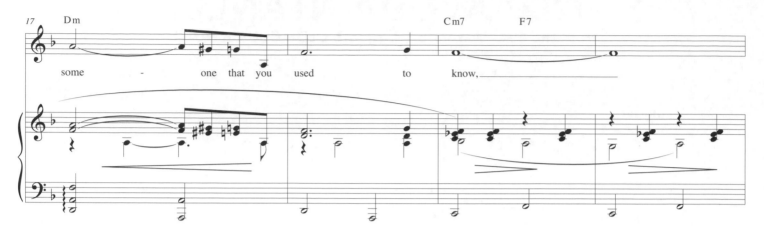

some - one that you used to know,_____

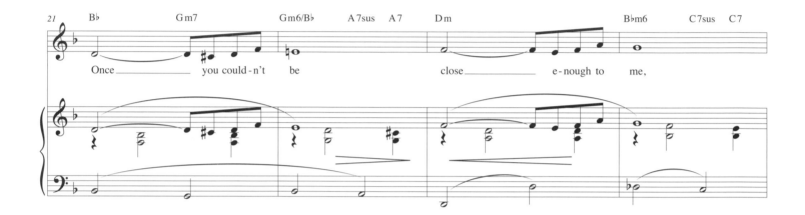

Once_____ you could - n't be close_____ e - nough to me,

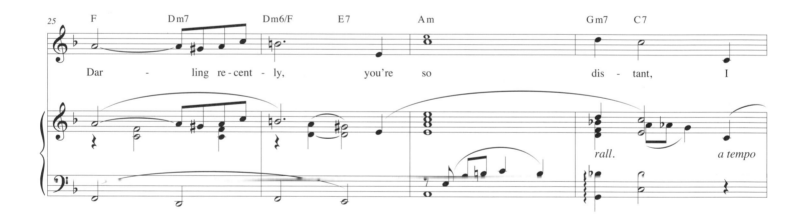

Dar - ling re - cent - ly, you're so dis - tant, I

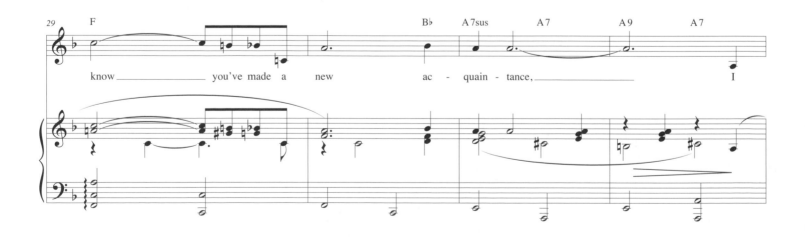

know_____ you've made a new ac - quain - tance,_____ I

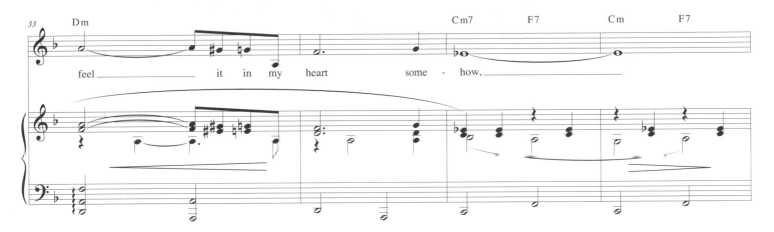

feel _____ it in my heart some - how, _____

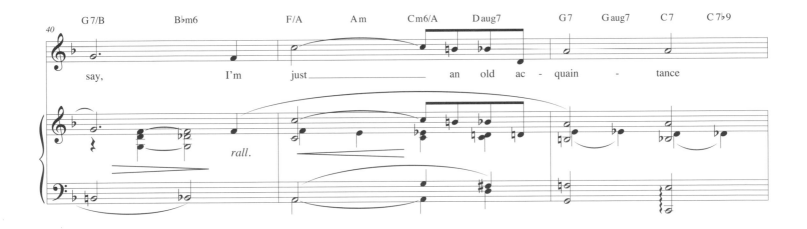

Nev - er thought the day would come _____ when I would

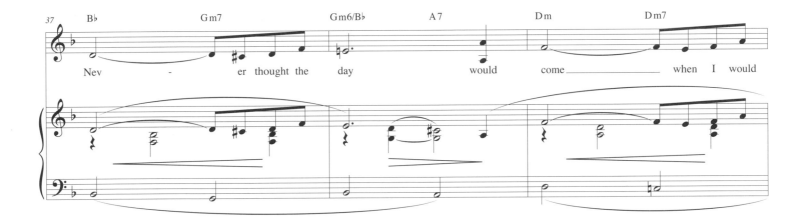

say, I'm just _____ an old ac - quain - tance

rall.

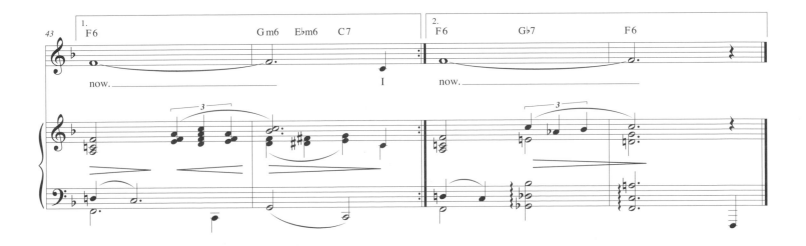

now. I now. _____

MANY DREAMS AGO

from the 1954 Paramount Picture ELEPHANT WALK

Music by FRANZ WAXMAN
Words by MACK DAVID

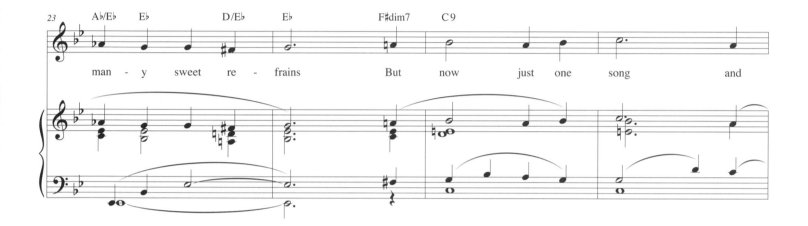

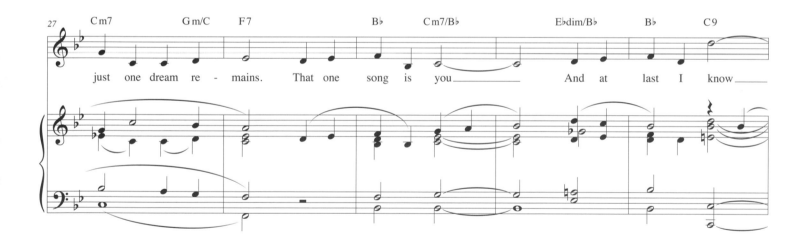

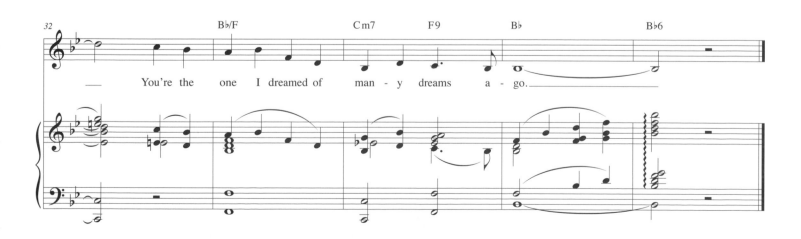

MY GEISHA – MAIN THEME

from the 1961 Paramount Picture MY GEISHA

By FRANZ WAXMAN

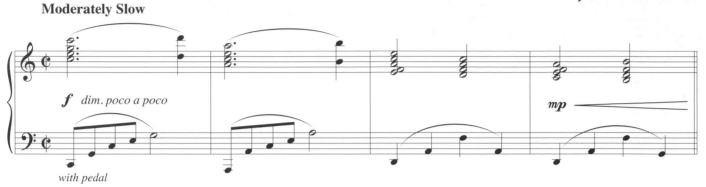

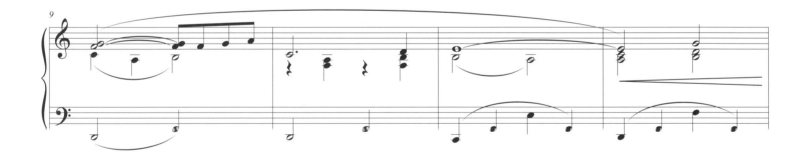

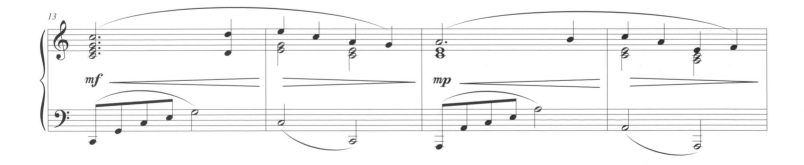

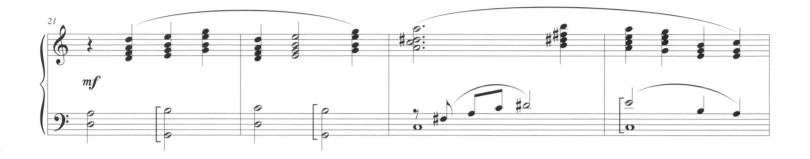

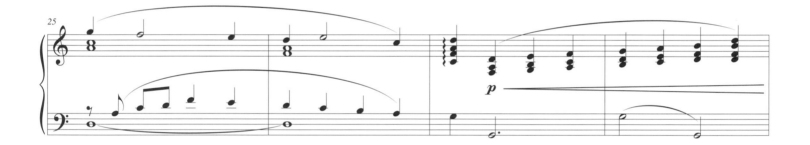

THE NUN'S STORY

from the 1959 Warner Bros. Picture THE NUN'S STORY

By FRANZ WAXMAN
Arranged by Patrick Russ

Maestoso ($\quarternote$ = c. 60)

pedal ad lib., wash

OBJECTIVE, BURMA!
(March)
from the 1945 Warner Bros. Picture OBJECTIVE, BURMA!

By FRANZ WAXMAN
Arranged by Patrick Russ

March (♩ = 120)

OUR WORRIES ARE OVER
(La crise est finie)
from the 1934 film LA CRISE EST FINIE

Music by FRANZ WAXMAN and JEAN LENOIR
Original Lyrics by MAX COLPET and JEAN LENOIR
English Lyrics by JEREMY LAWRENCE
Arranged by Arnold Freed

Moderate Fox Trot

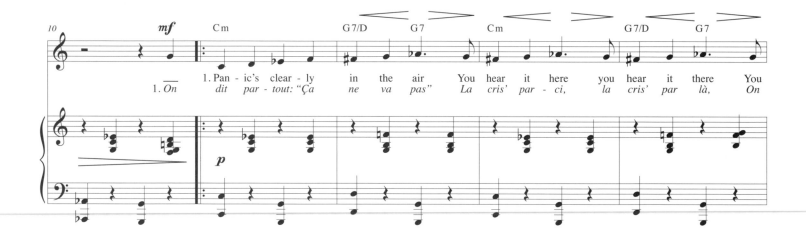

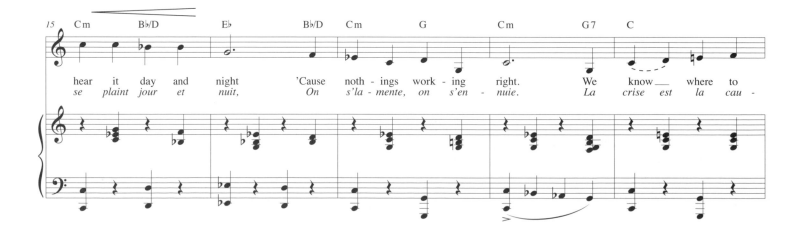

1. Pan - ic's clear - ly in the air You hear it here you hear it there You
1. *On dit par - tout: "Ça ne va pas" La cris' par - ci, la cris' par là, On*

hear it day and night 'Cause noth - ings work - ing right. We know____ where to
se plaint jour et nuit, On s'la - mente, on s'en - nuie. La crise est la cau -

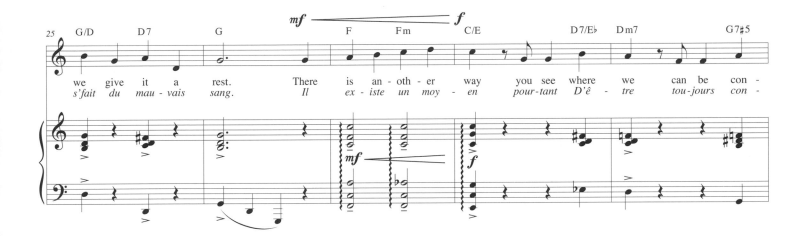

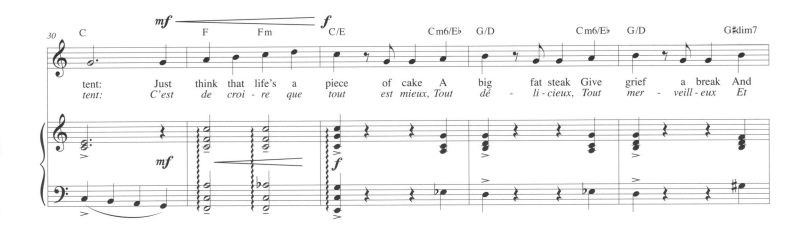

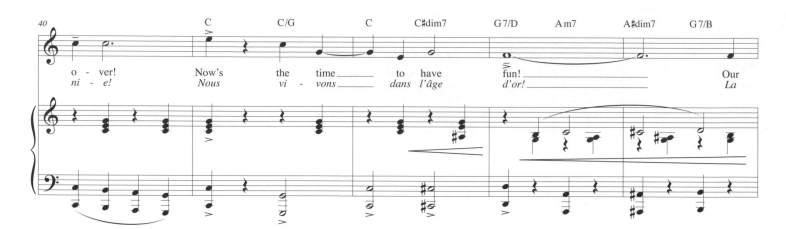

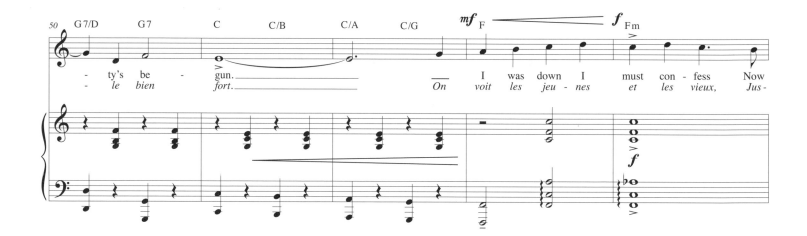

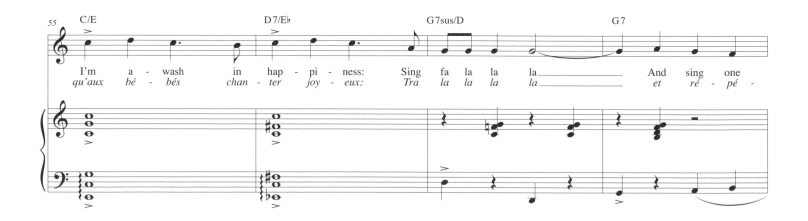

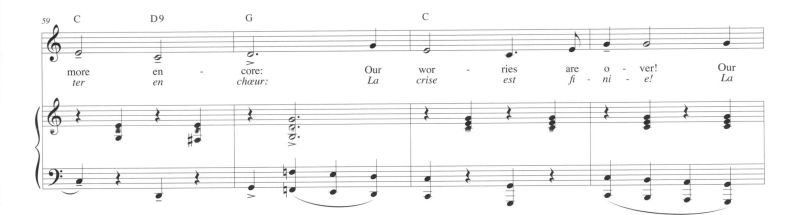

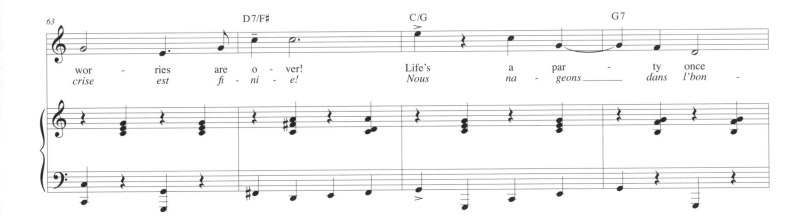

2. One whispers once upon a time
   We lived like kings life was sublime
   And everything was free
   Life was good as it could be.
   Both rich and poor alike would stroll
   On foot - of course - with no great goal
   Some free time free from care
   A breath of cool fresh air.
   Now no one walks they drive in-stead
   Polluting the fresh air with lead.
   In clubs they spin the roulette wheel
   It makes them feel their wealth is real
   While they get deep in debt.

3. Optimists we all must be
   The opposite brings misery
   Why chew on gloom and doom
   And seek an early tomb?
   Once all your taxes have been paid
   You've nothing left don't be afraid
   Don't fret and feel bereft
   Get rid of all that's left.
   For naked we came in the world
   So why not be unfurled
   Your lack of work may prove to be
   A sexy opportunity
   So sing orgasmicly:

2. *On soupire, on dit: autre fois*
   On était heureux comm' des rois
   La vie était pour rien
   Et l'on vivait si bien.
   Le purotin comm' le rentier
   Se baladait toujours à pied
   L'été, pour prendr' le frais,
   Dans l'train, suait à peu d'frais.
   Maintenant les p'tits comm' les gros
   Ne roulent qu'en auto
   Dans les cercles, les casinos,
   L'or coule à flots Rien n'est trop beau
   Car, disonsle bien haut:

3. *Il faut toujours être optimiste*
   Ça vaut bien mieux que d'être triste
   Pour-quoi broyer du noir
   Et perdre tout espoir.
   Le percepteur et ses impôts
   Nous laissent tout juste la peau
   Soyons joyeux et nus,
   Sans rentes ni rev'nus
   Si l'on chôme pendant le jour
   La nuit, on fait l'amour.
   On travailleau repeuplement
   Et les amants bien gentiment
   Redisent tendrement:

POVERTY IS EVERYWHERE
(So ein Dalles geht über alles!)
from the 1932 film DAS MÄDEL VON MONTPARNASSE

Music by FRANZ WAXMAN
Original Lyrics by ROBERT GILBERT
English Lyrics by JEREMY LAWRENCE
Arranged by Arnold Freed

Fox Trot tempo - Allegro moderato

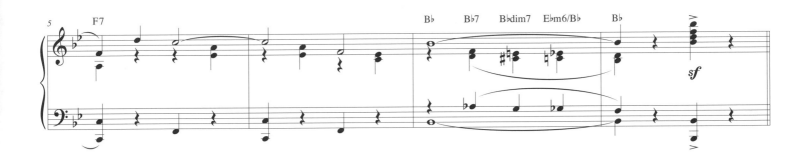

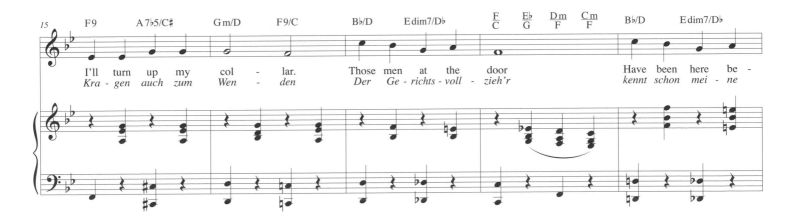

1. Don't you wor-ry kids / Though I'm on the skids / I won't scream and hol-ler
1. *Kin - der, mir geht's gut!* / *Ich hab' noch 'nen Mut,* / *Hand-schuh an den Hän - den,*

I'll turn up my col-lar. / Those men at the door / Have been here be-
Kra - gen auch zum Wen - den / *Der Ge - richts-voll - zieh'r* / *kennt schon mei - ne*

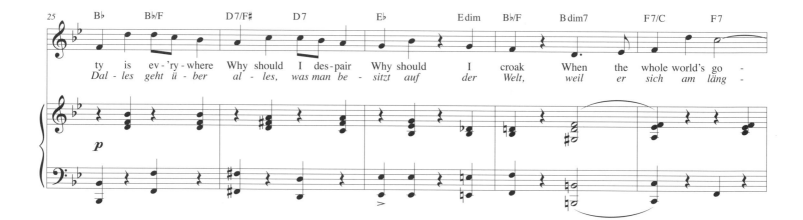

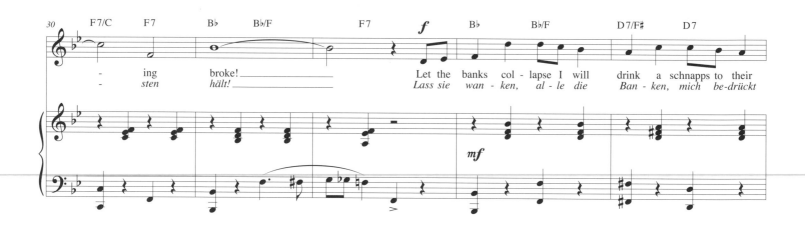

Climb-ing to the top is oh so stress - ful Job-less fi-nal-ly I feel suc-
Mir kann, gott-sei-dank, nicht viel pas-sie - ren, denn ich hab' nur Schul-den zu ver-

cess - ful! Pov-er-ty is ev-'ry-where Why should I des-pair Why should I
lie - ren! So ein Dal-les geht ü-ber al-les, was man be-sitzt auf der

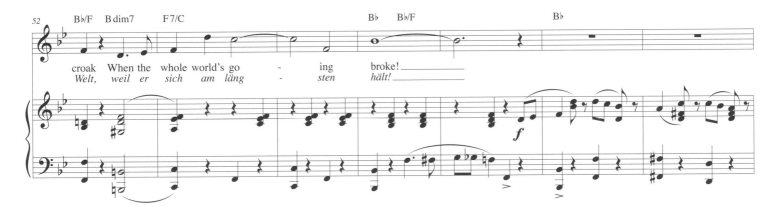

croak When the whole world's go - ing broke! ____
Welt, weil er sich am läng - sten hält! ____

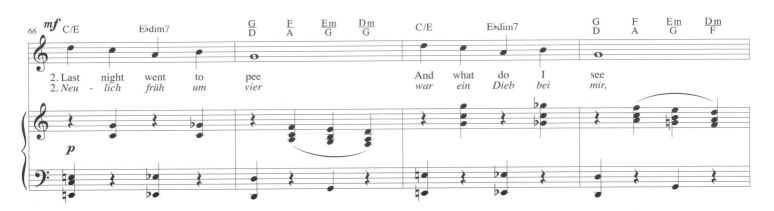

2. Last night went to pee And what do I see
2. Neu-lich früh um vier war ein Dieb bei mir,

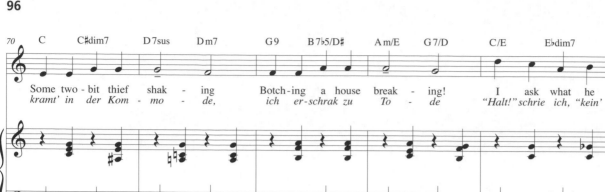

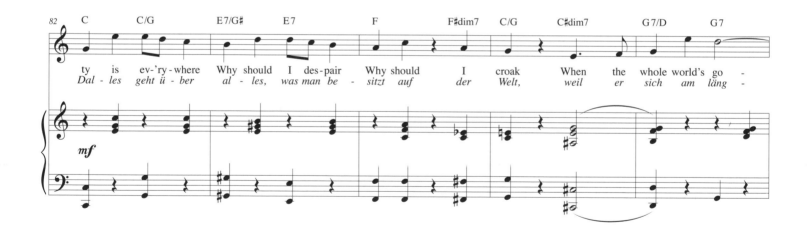

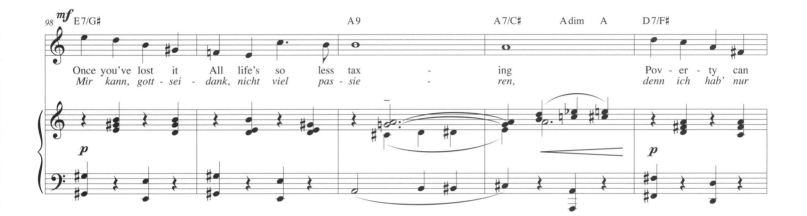

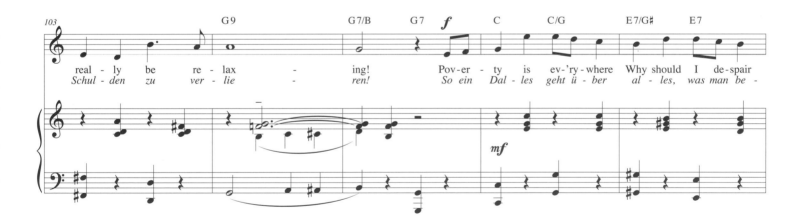

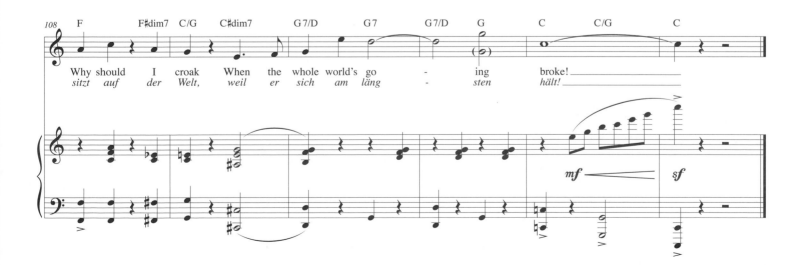

A PENNY'S WORTH OF LOVIN'

(Für 'nen Groschen Liebe)

from the 1932 film SCAMPOLO, A CHILD OF THE STREET

Music by FRANZ WAXMAN
Original Lyrics by MAX COLPET
English Lyrics by JEREMY LAWRENCE
Arranged by Arnold Freed

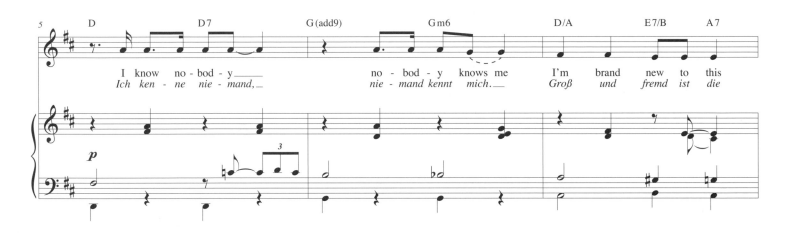

I know no-bod-y___ no-bod-y knows me. I'm brand new to this
Ich ken - ne nie-mand,___ nie - mand kennt mich.___ Groß und fremd ist die

town. I love no-bod-y___ no-bod-y loves me
Stadt. Ich lie - be nie - mand,___ nie - mand liebt mich.___

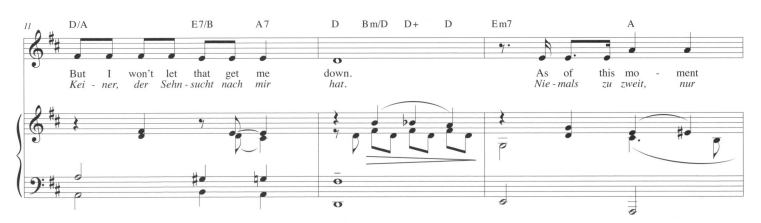

But I won't let that get me down. As of this mo - ment
Kei - ner, der Sehn - sucht nach mir hat. Nie - mals zu zweit, nur

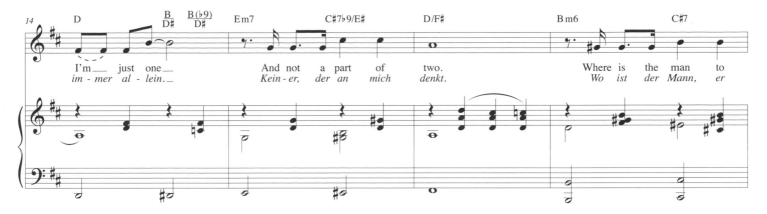

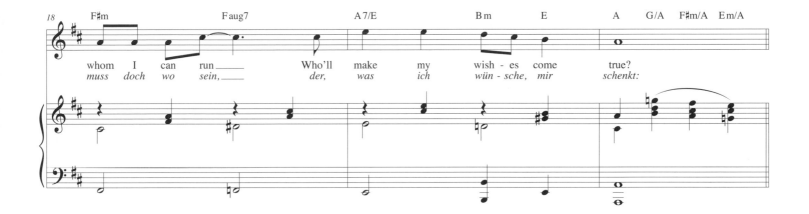

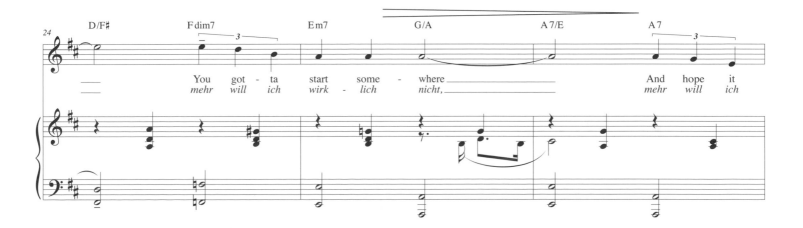

grows from there._____
wirk - lich nicht._____

A pen - ny's worth of lov - in'_____
Für 'nen Gro - schen Lie - be,_____

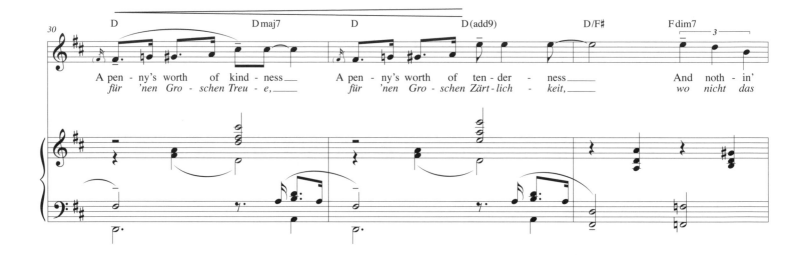

A pen - ny's worth of kind - ness_____ A pen - ny's worth of ten - der - ness_____ And noth - in'
für 'nen Gro - schen Treu - e,_____ für 'nen Gro - schen Zärt - lich - keit,_____ wo nicht das

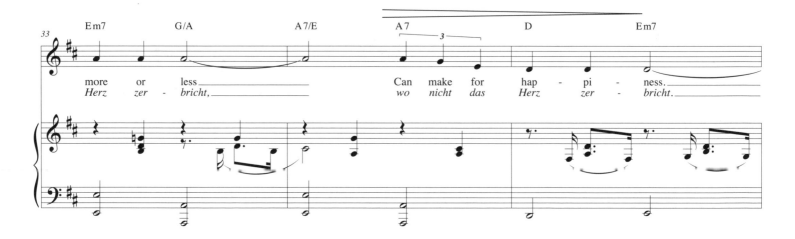

more or less_____ Can make for hap - pi - ness._____
Herz zer - bricht,_____ wo nicht das Herz zer - bricht._____

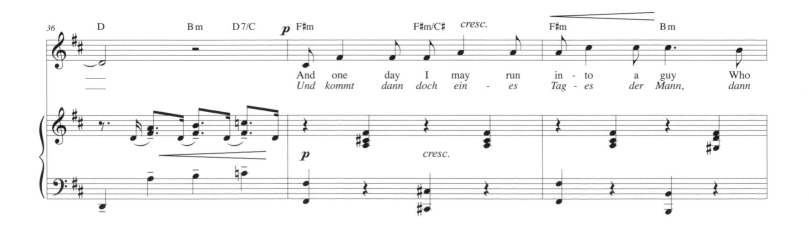

And one day I may run in - to a guy, Who
Und kommt dann doch ein - es Tag - es der Mann, dann

makes me feel qui - et and still, And my eyes will ask him to
bin ich ganz klein und ganz still, dann se - he ich ihn vol - ler

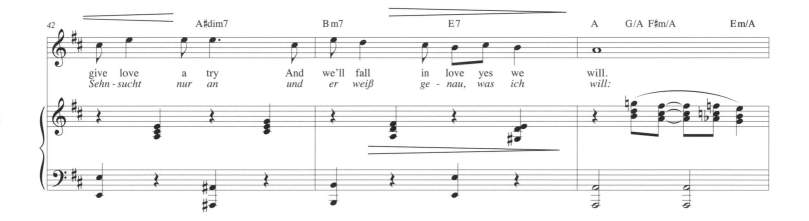

give love a try And we'll fall in love yes we will.
Sehn - sucht nur an und er weiß ge - nau, was ich will:

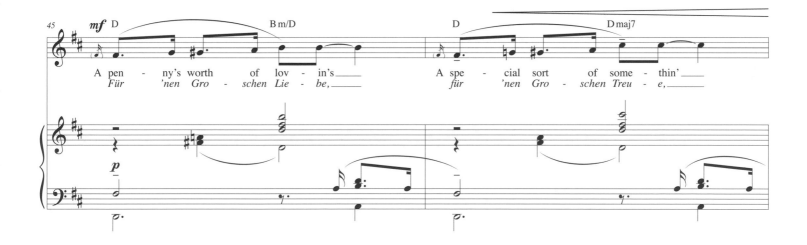

A pen - ny's worth of lov - in's, A spe - cial sort of some - thin'____
Für 'nen Gro - schen Lie - be,____ für 'nen Gro - schen Treu - e,____

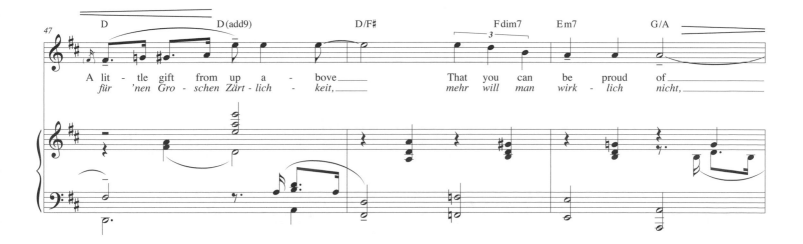

A lit - tle gift from up a - bove____ That you can be proud of____
für 'nen Gro - schen Zärt - lich - keit,____ mehr will man wirk - lich nicht,____

So fall in love!
mehr will man nicht!

I'm not na - ïve I know life is - n't fair. I've had my fair share of bad
Und kommt dann doch ein - es Tag - es der Mann, dann bin ich ganz klein und ganz

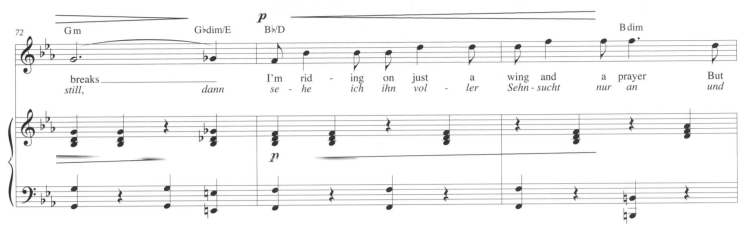

breaks ___ I'm rid-ing on just a wing and a prayer But
still, *dann* *se - he* *ich* *ihn* *vol - ler* *Sehn - sucht* *nur* *an* *und*

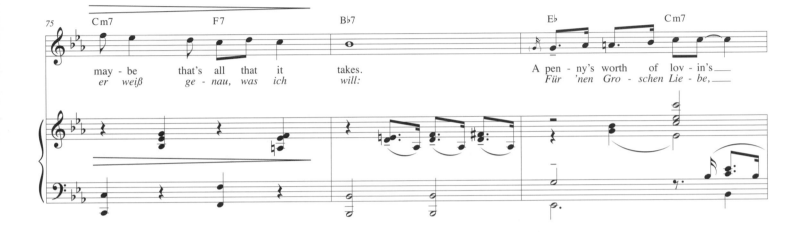

may - be that's all that it takes. A pen-ny's worth of lov-in's ___
er *weiß* *ge - nau,* *was* *ich* *will:* *Für* *'nen* *Gro - schen* *Lie - be,* ___

A bet that's al - most cer - tain ___ Heads or tails you're bound to win ___ So give that
für *'nen* *Gro - schen* *Treu - e,* ___ *für* *'nen* *Gro - schen* *Zärt - lich - keit,* ___ *mehr* *will* *man*

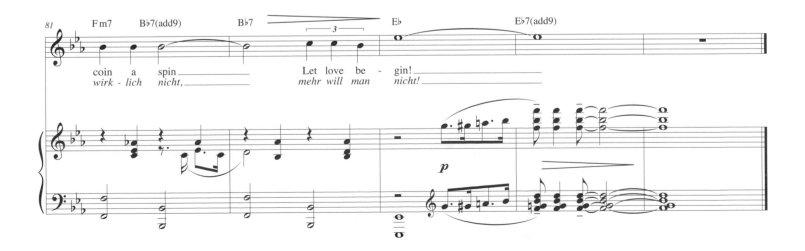

coin a spin ___ Let love be - gin! ___
wirk - lich *nicht,* ___ *mehr* *will* *man* *nicht!* ___

THEME FROM
THE PHILADELPHIA STORY

from the 1940 MGM Picture THE PHILADELPHIA STORY

By FRANZ WAXMAN
Arranged by Patrick Russ

With swagger (♩ = 84)

ROSANNA
from the 1962 20th Century Fox Picture
HEMINGWAY'S ADVENTURES OF A YOUNG MAN

By FRANZ WAXMAN

Molto rubato

SAY THAT YOU LOVE ME
(Sag' mir einmal: "Ich liebe Dich")

Music by FRANZ WAXMAN
Original Text by FRANZ SCHUBERT
English Lyrics by JEREMY LAWRENCE
Arranged by G. Gürsch

Moderato (♩ = 80)

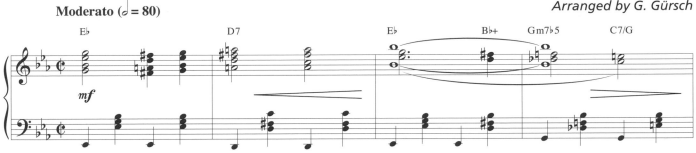

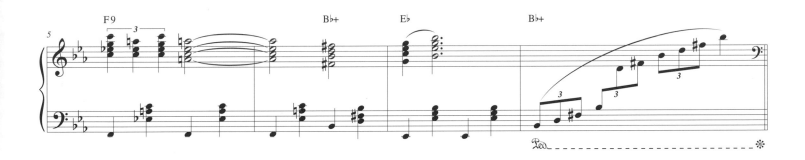

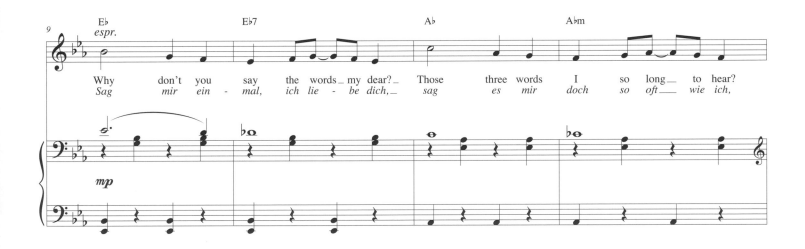

Why don't you say the words_ my dear?_ Those three words I so long_ to hear?
Sag mir ein- mal, ich lie- be dich,_ sag es mir doch so oft_ wie ich,

Dar - ling,_____ say you love me.
Lieb - ling,_____ dann wär ich froh.

What does all of my lov - ing lack? Can you tell me what holds__ you back?
Sei ein - mal nur so treu__ wie ich, Sag ein - mal nur, ich lie - be dich,

Dar - ling,_____ say that you love me.
Lieb - ling,_____ dann wär ich glück - lich.

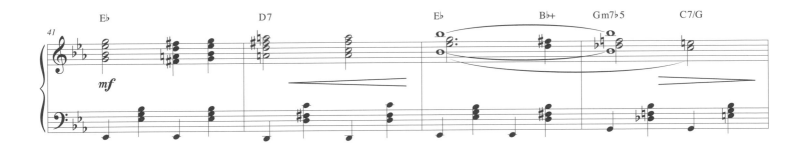

SOMETHING IN MY HEART

from the 1935 Universal Pictures film THE AFFAIR OF SUSAN

Music by FRANZ WAXMAN
Words by E.Y. HARBURG

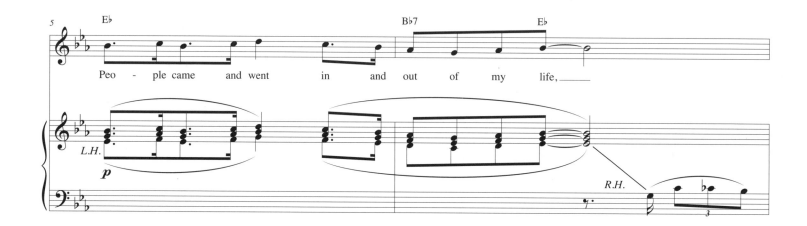

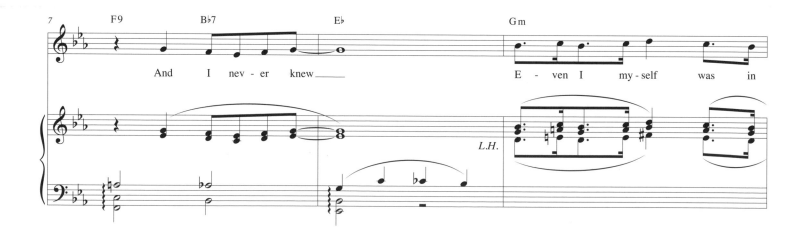

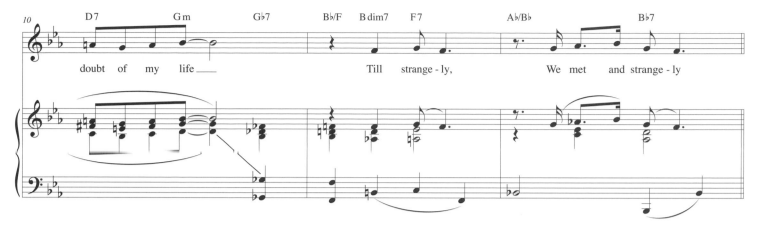

doubt of my life___ Till strange - ly, We met and strange - ly

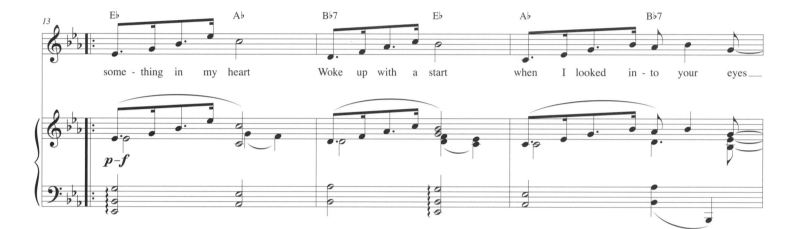

some - thing in my heart Woke up with a start when I looked in - to your eyes___

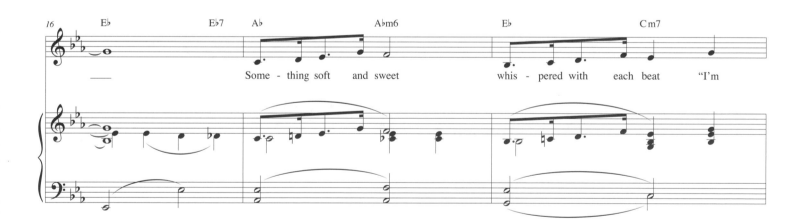

___ Some - thing soft and sweet whis - pered with each beat "I'm

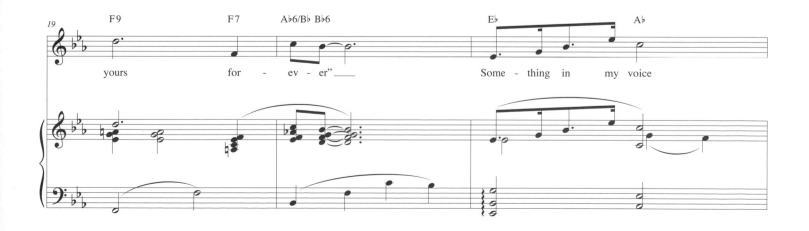

yours for - ev - er"___ Some - thing in my voice

Want - ed to re - joice When your glance had an - swered mine _____

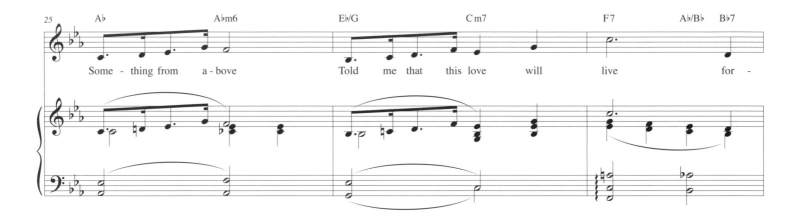

Some - thing from a - bove Told me that this love will live for -

ev - er _____ Life had seemed a dark and dream - less night here with - out you.

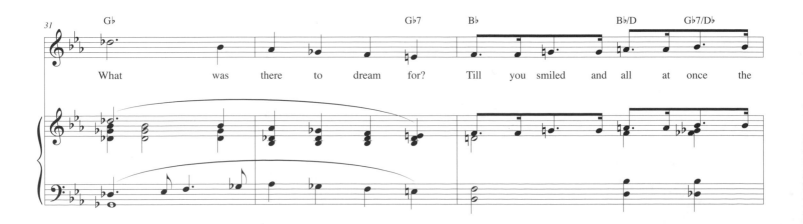

What was there to dream for? Till you smiled and all at once the

THE SONG OF RUTH

from the 1960 20th Century Fox Picture THE STORY OF RUTH

Music by FRANZ WAXMAN
Lyrics by PAUL FRANCIS WEBSTER

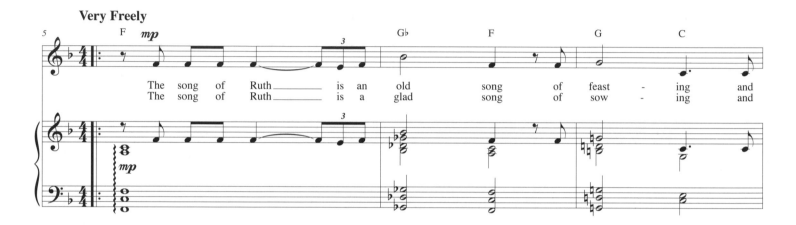

The song of Ruth_____ is an old song of feast - ing and
The song of Ruth_____ is a glad song of sow - ing and

fast - ing, The song of Ruth_____ is a bold song of
reap - ing, The song of Ruth_____ is a sad song of

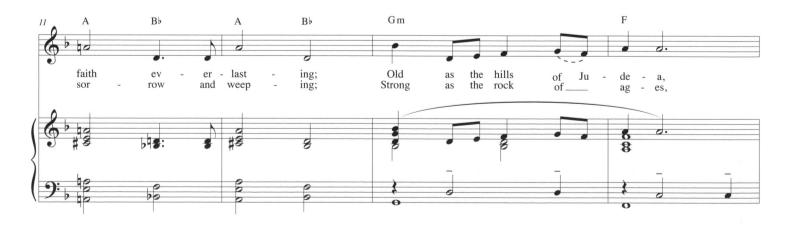

faith ev - er - last - ing; Old as the hills of Ju - de - a,
sor - row and weep - ing; Strong as the rock of_____ ag - es,

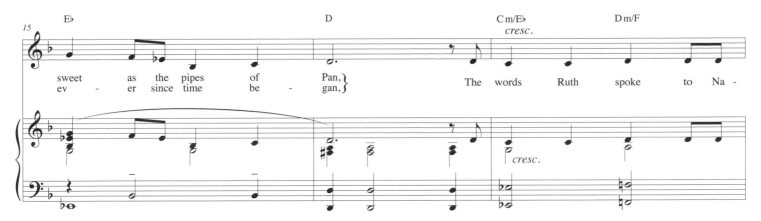

sweet as the pipes of Pan,} The words Ruth spoke to Na-
ev - er since time be - gan,}

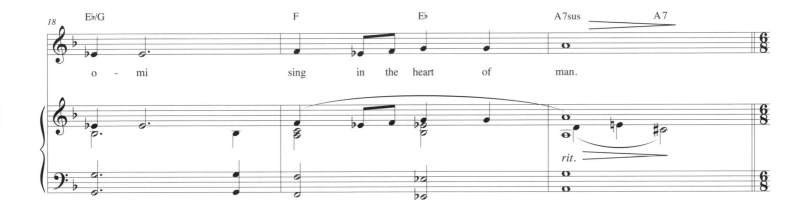

o - mi sing in the heart of man.

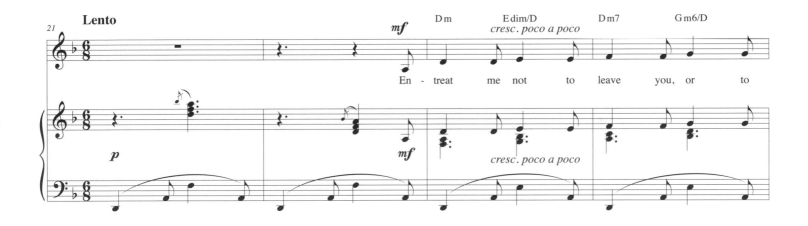

En - treat me not to leave you, or to

keep from fol - low-ing you;____ For where you go, I shall

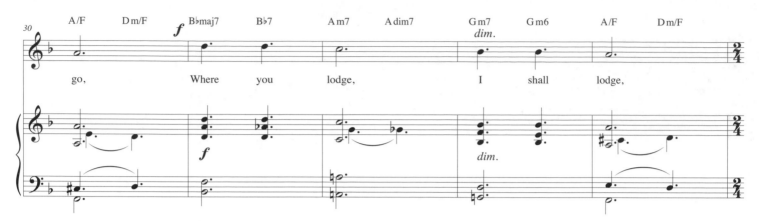

SPICE IT UP!
(Ich hab' so was im Blut)
from the 1932 film PAPRIKA

Music by FRANZ WAXMAN
Original Lyrics by KURT SCHWABACH and MAX COLPET
English Lyrics by JEREMY LAWRENCE
Arranged by Arnold Freed

Lively con spirito

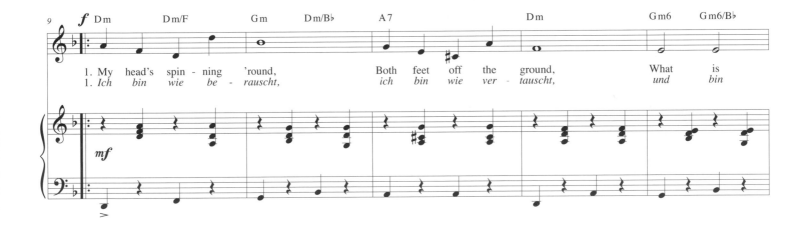

1. My head's spin-ning 'round, Both feet off the ground, What is
1. *Ich bin wie be - rauscht, ich bin wie ver - tauscht, und bin*

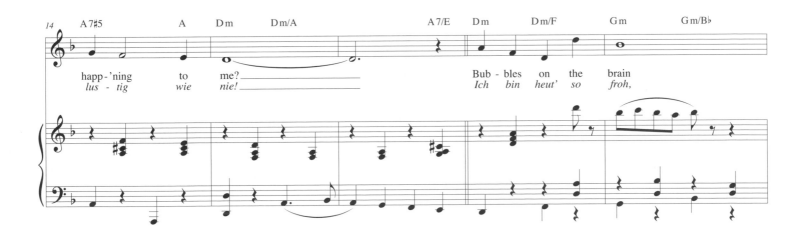

happ-'ning to me? Bub-bles on the brain
lus - tig wie nie! Ich bin heut' so froh,

Feel a bit in-sane, I'm in ec-sta-sy._____ It
heu-te ist mir so, *Ich weiß selbst nicht wie._____* *Ich*

is-n't booze or coke, Or ma-ri-jua-na smoke, It's just a dash of
hab' so was im Blut, *ich hab' so was im Blut,* *ich glaub', das ist der*

good old fash-ioned pap-ri-ka, no joke! Oh I'm the cat's me-ow, I
Pa-pri-ka und Pap-ri-ka ist gut! *Heut' muss et-was ge-scheh'n,* *heut'*

found the se-cret now, Just take a whiff of pap-ri-ka, A lit-tle whiff and
hab' ich sol-chen Mut, *ich glaub', das ist der Pap-ri-ka, der Pap-ri-ka im*

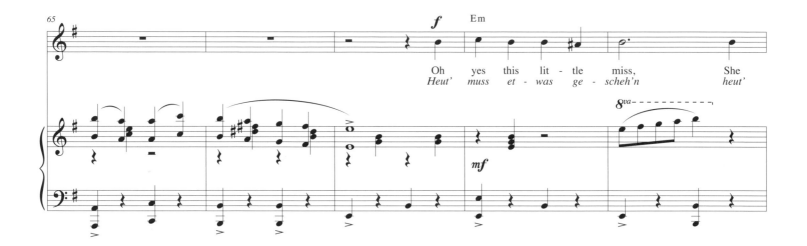

Oh yes this lit - tle miss, She
Heut' muss et - was ge - scheh'n heut'

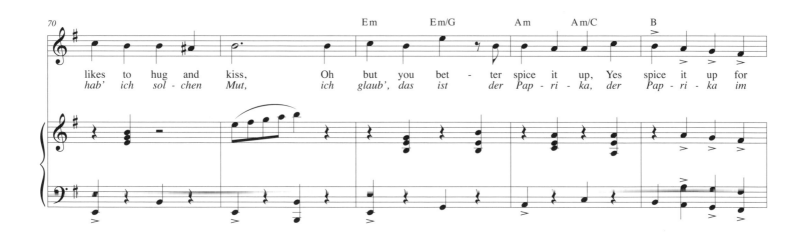

likes to hug and kiss, Oh but you bet - ter spice it up, Yes spice it up for
hab' ich sol - chen Mut, ich glaub', das ist der Pap - ri - ka, der Pap - ri - ka im

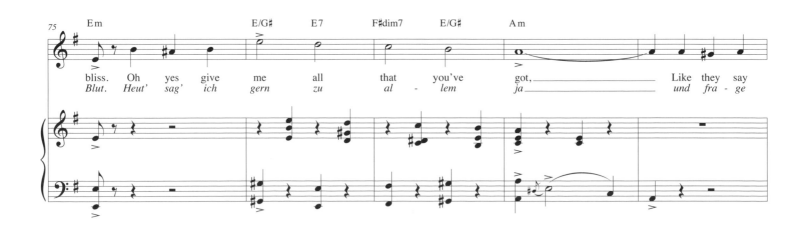

bliss. Oh yes give me all that you've got,_____ Like they say
Blut. Heut' sag' ich gern zu al - lem ja_____ und fra - ge

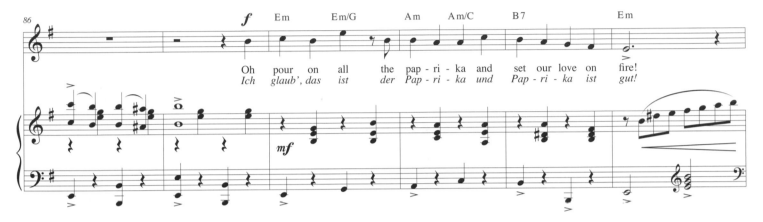

2. Make my sour cream,
   A spicy little dream,
   My defenses will fall.
   If you do it right,
   You can spend the night,
   This girl wants it all.

2. *Kommt der richt'ge Mann,*
   der gut küssen kann,
   dann sagt keine Frau nein,
   sondern denkt sich bloß:
   Was ist mit mir los,
   was kann das bloß sein?

SONG OF THE EMPRESS
(Lied der Kaiserin)
from the 1933 film ICH UND DIE KAISERIN

Music by FRANZ WAXMAN
Original Lyrics by ROBERT LIEBMANN and WALTER REISCH
English Lyrics by JEREMY LAWRENCE
Arranged by Arnold Freed

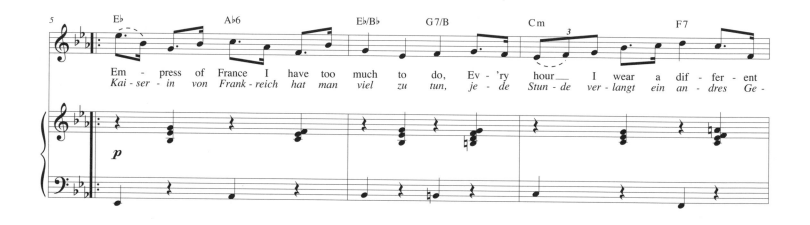

Em - press of France I have too much to do, Ev - 'ry hour___ I wear a dif - fer - ent
Kai - ser - in von Frank - reich hat man viel zu tun, je - de Stun - de ver - langt ein an - dres Ge -

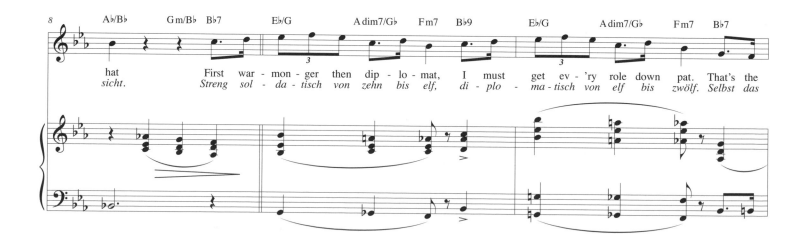

hat First war - mon - ger then dip - lo - mat, I must get ev - 'ry role down pat. That's the
sicht. Streng sol - da - tisch von zehn bis elf, di - plo - ma - tisch von elf bis zwölf. Selbst das

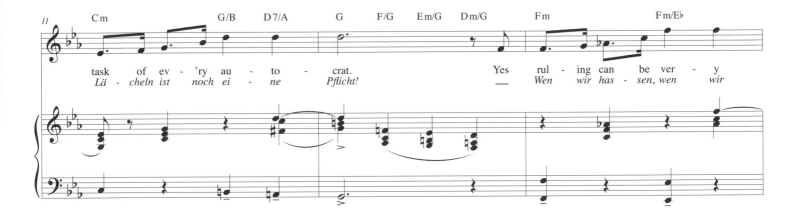

task of ev-'ry au-to- crat. Yes rul -ing can be ver - y
Lä - cheln ist noch ei - ne Pflicht! Wen wir has - sen, wen wir

tax- ing. There's no time for just re - lax - ing. O but
lie - ben, al - les ist uns vor - ge - schrie - ben! A - ber

Sehr leicht und flott

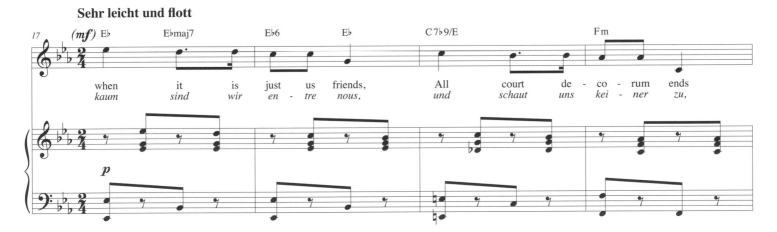

when it is just us friends, All court de - co - rum ends
kaum sind wir en - tre nous, und schaut uns kei - ner zu,

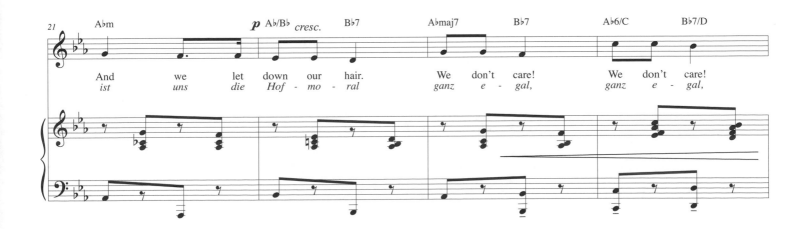

And we let down our hair. We don't care! We don't care!
ist uns die Hof - mo - ral ganz e - gal, ganz e - gal,

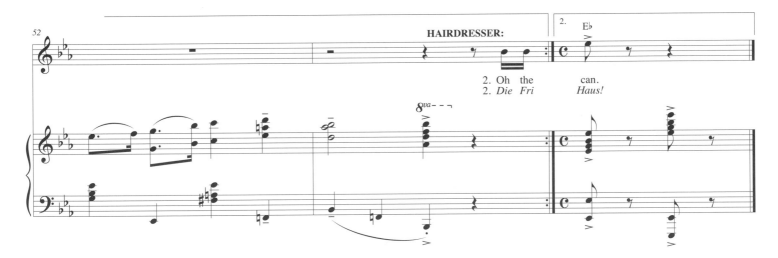

2. Oh the hair-style of the Empress changes ev'ry hour,
   Ev'ry role must be coiffed quite differently.
   Cold severe hair from two to three.
   Next demonic she wants to be.
   And then Madam de Pompadour is she.
   She'll forever be remembered
   For the ringlets I engendered.
   O but after formalities
   She loves frivolities
   Down fall her lovely curls
   As she whirls. As she whirls.
   She lets her hair just fly,
   While she is kicking high.
   She grabs each chance she gets to dance the can-can when she can.
   She lets her hair just fly,
   While she is kicking high.
   She grabs each chance she gets to dance the can-can when she can.

2. *Die Friseuse einer Kaiserin hat viel zu tun,*
   jede Stunde verlangt 'ne andre Frisur.
   Streng harmonisch von eins bis zwei,
   leicht dämonisch von zwei bis drei,
   und am Abend à la Pompadour!
   Jede Locke, die ich richte,
   kommt mal in die Weltgeschichte!
   Aber kaum sind wir entre nous,
   und schaut uns keiner zu,
   ist uns die Hofmoral ganz egal, ganz egal,
   und in den Fingern juckts, und in den Beinen zuckts,
   plötzlich bricht der Cancan aus im kaiserlichen Haus!
   Und in den Fingern juckts, und in den Beinen zuckts,
   plötzlich bricht der Cancan aus im kaiserlichen Haus!

SUNRISE AT CAMPOBELLO

from the 1960 Warner Bros. Picture SUNRISE AT CAMPOBELLO

By FRANZ WAXMAN
Arranged by Patrick Russ

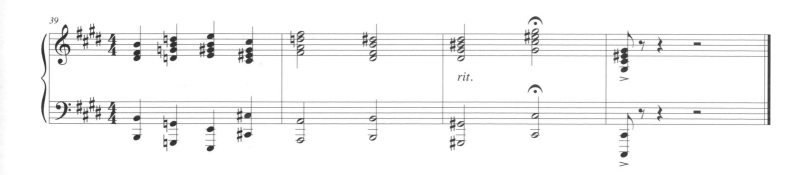

SUNSET BOULEVARD

from the 1950 Paramount Motion Picture SUNSET BOULEVARD

By FRANZ WAXMAN
Arranged by Patrick Russ and Paul Henning

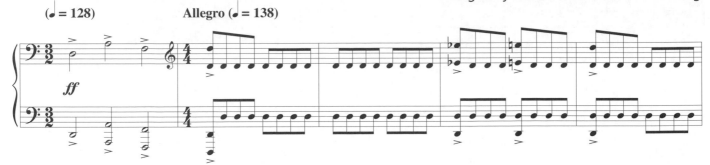

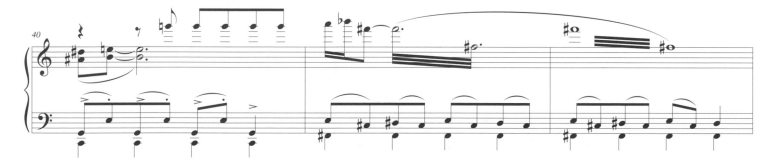

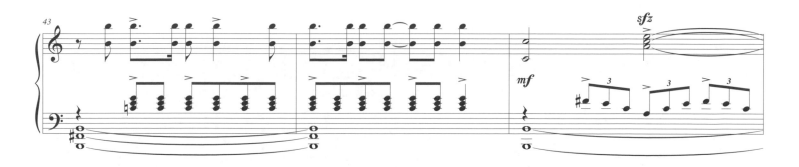

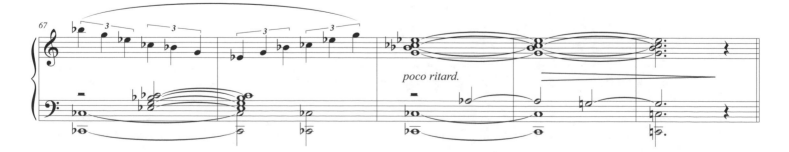

Meno mosso (♩ = 66)

Swing eighths, slightly (♩ = 65 - 70)

Straight eighths now (♩ = 65 - 70)

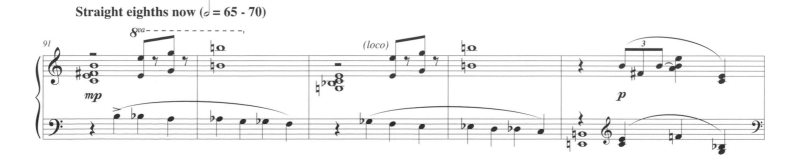

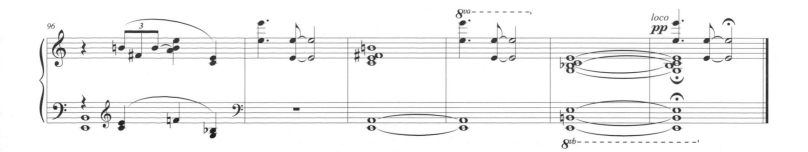

THIS IS MY LOVE
from the 1954 RKO Radio Picture THIS IS MY LOVE

Words by HUGH BROOKE
Music by FRANZ WAXMAN

Moderato, with feeling

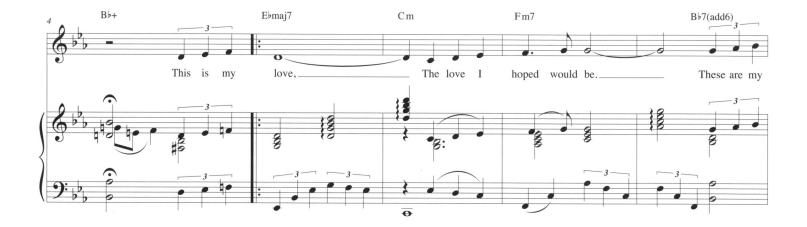

TONIGHT MY LOVE

from the 1951 Paramount Motion Picture A PLACE IN THE SUN

Words by JAY LIVINGSTON and RAY EVANS
Music by FRANZ WAXMAN

Slowly With Much Expression

I've no de - sire to be knee-deep in treas - ure; I don't as -

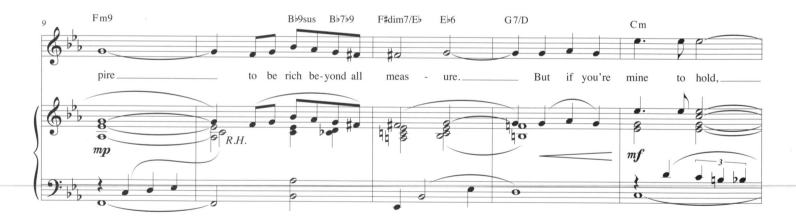

pire to be rich be-yond all meas - ure. But if you're mine to hold,

to let my arms en - fold, I'll have my share of gold and a place in the

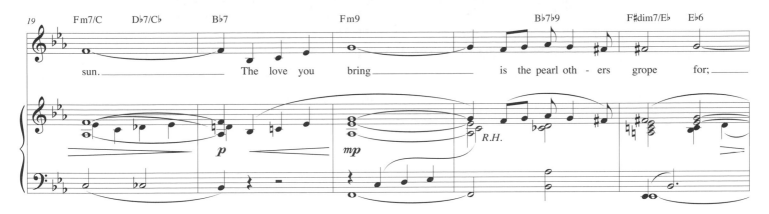

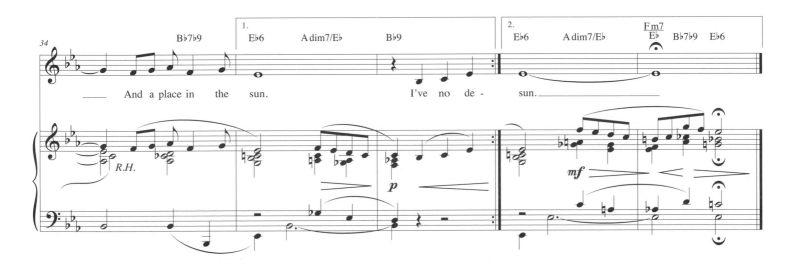

TRUE LOVE IS WAITING
(Ewige Liebe gibt's nur im Roman!)
from the 1930 film DAS KABINETT DES DR. LARIFARI

Music by FRANZ WAXMAN
Original Lyrics by ROBERT GILBERT and ARMIN ROBINSON
English Lyrics by JEREMY LAWRENCE
Arranged by Arnold Freed

Waltz tempo, moderato (in 1)

1. Don't you dare, don't swear you'll love me for e - ter - ni - ty,
1. *Schwör' mir nicht, du liebst nur mich bis in die E - wig - keit,*

—— Love don't last that long. —— For to - night our
—— *denn ich weiß Be - scheid: —— Heut' bin ich die*

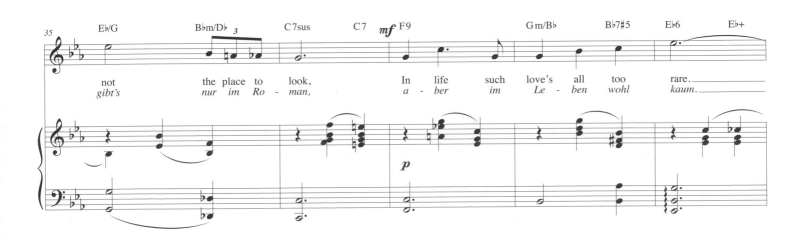

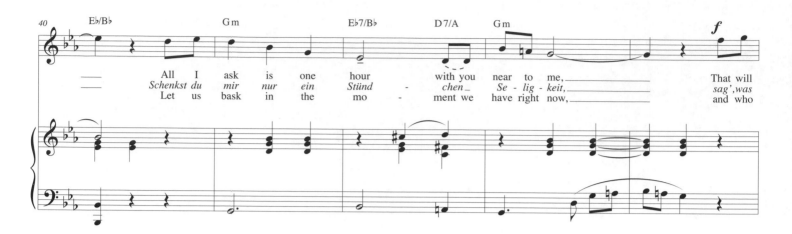

All I ask is one hour with you near to me,_____ That will
Schenkst du mir nur ein Stünd - chen_ Se - lig - keit,_____ sag',was
Let us bask in the mo - ment we have right now,_____ and who

last me for all of e - ter - ni - ty!_____ True love is
brauch' ich denn da_____ die E - wig - keit?!_____ E - wi - ge
knows we might just make it last some - how!_____

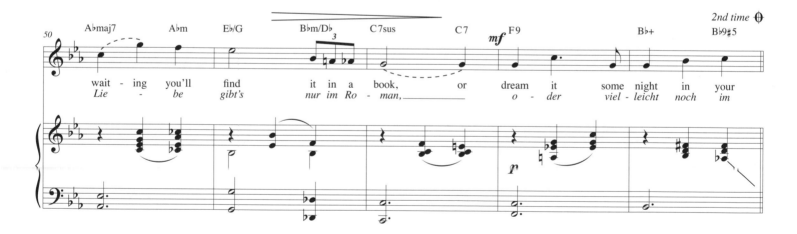

wait - ing you'll find it in a book, or dream it some night in your
Lie - be gibt's nur im Ro - man, o - der viel - leicht noch im

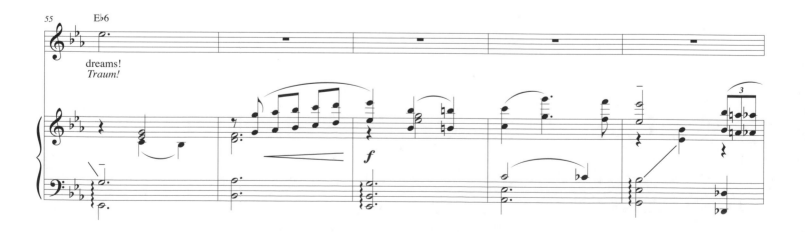

dreams!
Traum!

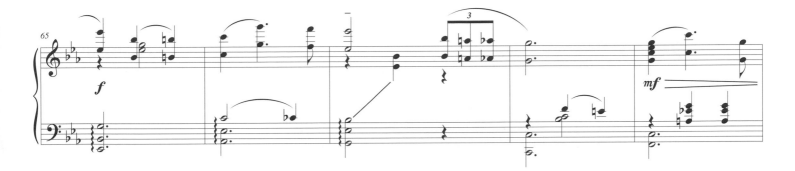

$\oplus$ CODA

2. Press your lips to mine one moment filled with tenderness,
I won't ask for more.
Knowing that our love won't last, I must confess,
Makes me love you more!

2. *Wenn dein Mund den meinen küsst, liegt in dem Augenblick
allerhöchstes Glück.
Dass dies' Glück nicht ewig ist, ich muss gesteh'n,
macht es g'rad so schön!*

3. Please don't say you'll be my love for all eternity,
I've heard that before.
Sure tonight I'm all your world, but while I sleep,
You'll slip out the door!

4. When your lips press mine, that kiss is momentary bliss,
kissing's awful nice.
As for me I'm happy for a short and quick
Taste of paradise!

WE JUST KNOW
(Sans un Mot)
from the 1934 film LA CRISE EST FINIE

Music by FRANZ WAXMAN
Original Lyrics by MAX COLPET and JEAN LENOIR
English Lyrics by JEREMY LAWRENCE
Arranged by Arnold Freed

Waltz tempo, moderato (in 1)

1. Our song has not one word, Si - lence is pre - ferred.
1. Chan - tant à l'u - nis - on, La mê - me chan - son.
2. Your pains I un - der - stand, They'll soft - en in my hand.

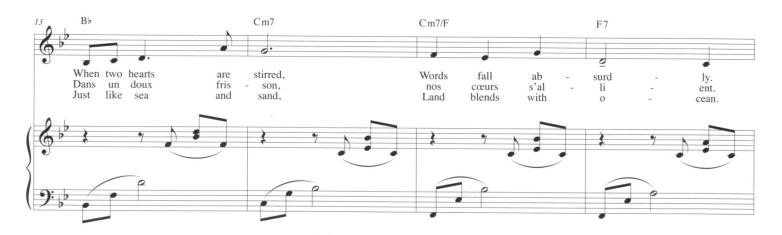

When two hearts are stirred, Words fall ab - surd - ly.
Dans un doux fris - son, nos cœurs s'al - li - ent.
Just like sea and sand, Land blends with o - cean.

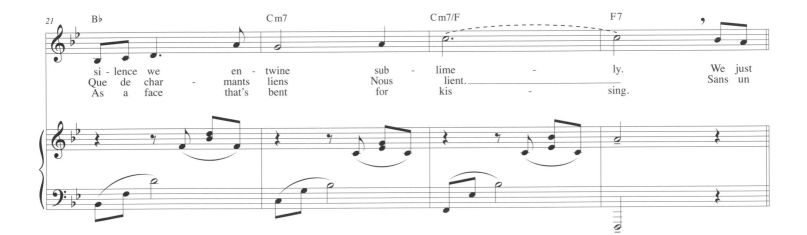

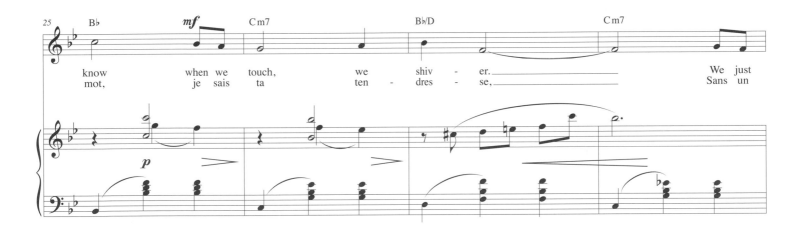

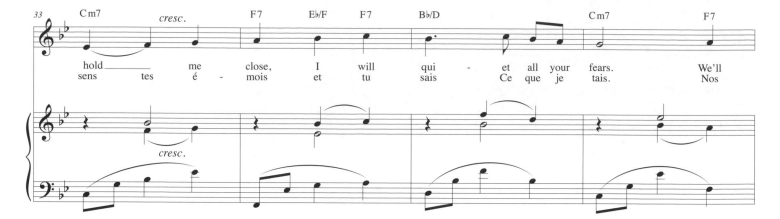

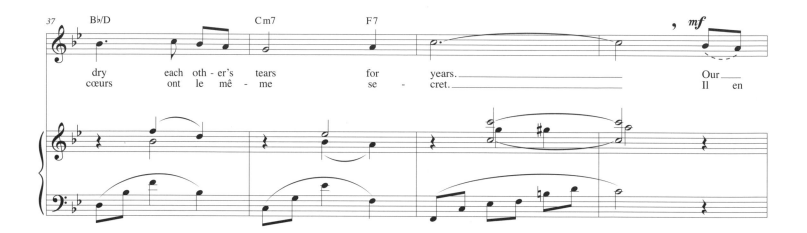

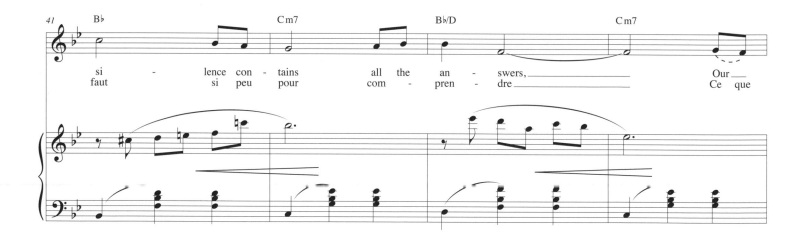

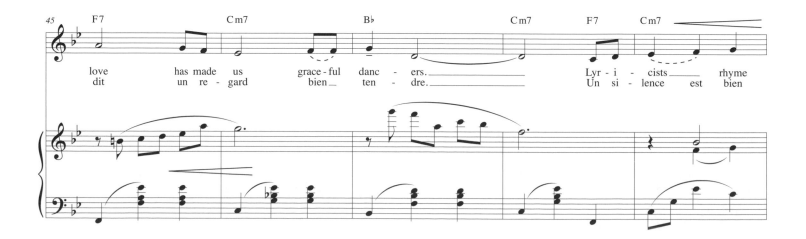

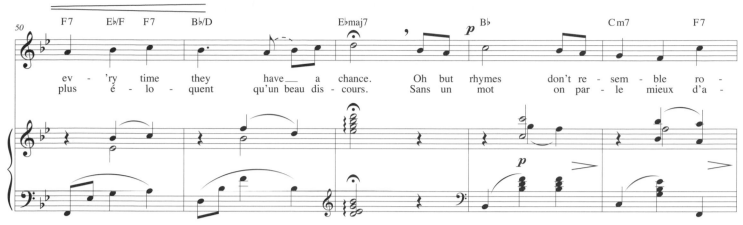

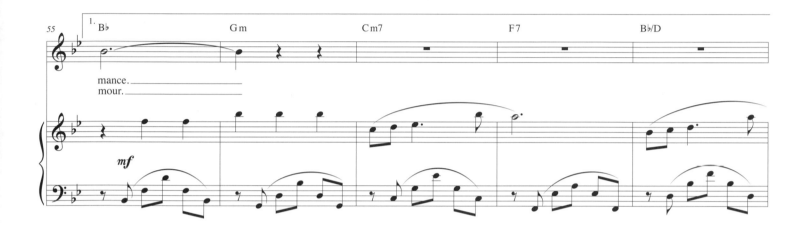

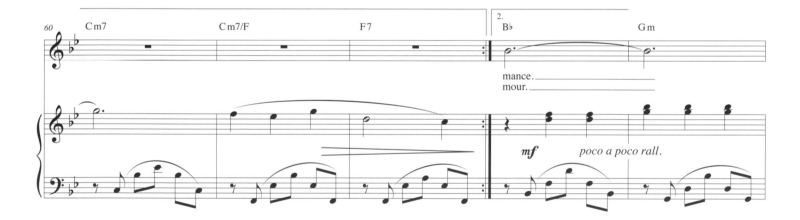

2. *Tu seras sans chagrin,*
   Si toujours ta main.
   Le long du chemin,
   Dans ma main reste.
   Les poêmes surfaits
   Au rythme parfait
   Ne vaudront jamais ce geste.

WHEN YOU LOVE
(Das Glück kommt nur einmal im Leben)
from the 1932 film PAPRIKA

Music by FRANZ WAXMAN
Original Lyrics by KURT SCHWABACH
English Lyrics by JEREMY LAWRENCE
Arranged by Arnold Freed

English Waltz (Andante moderato)

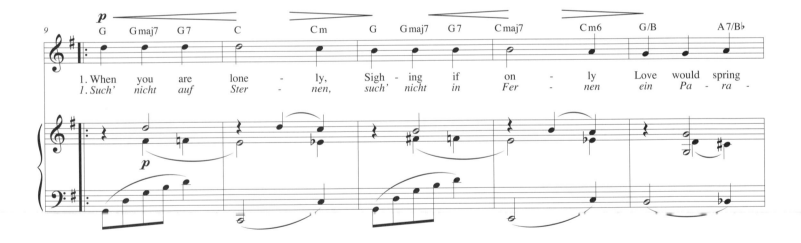

1. When you are lone - ly, Sigh - ing if on - ly Love would spring
1. *Such' nicht auf Ster - nen, such' nicht in Fer - nen ein Pa - ra -*

forth, and fall from the sky._____ Change how you're think - ing,
dies, das es gar nicht gibt. Glück - lich auf Er - den

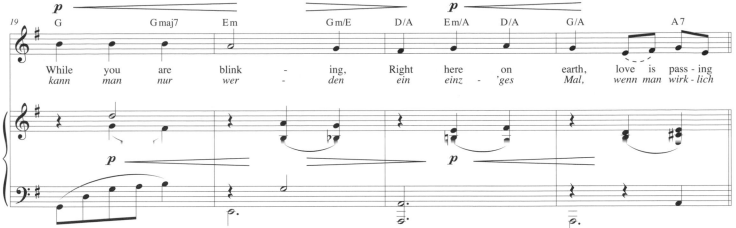

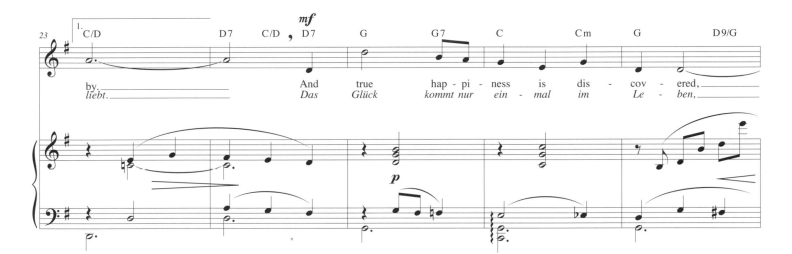

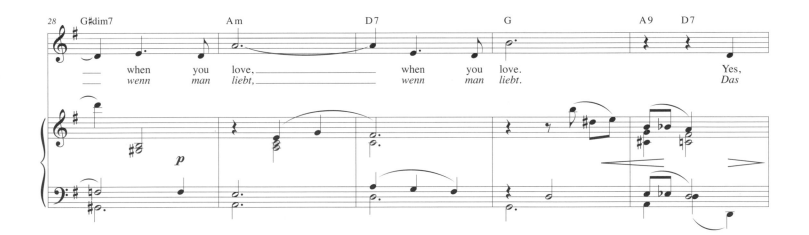

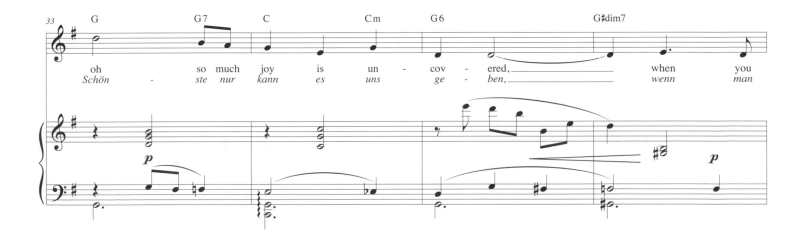

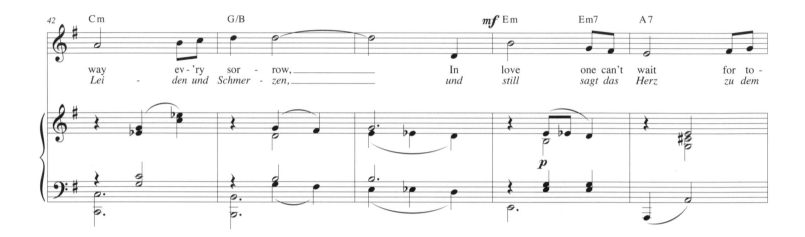

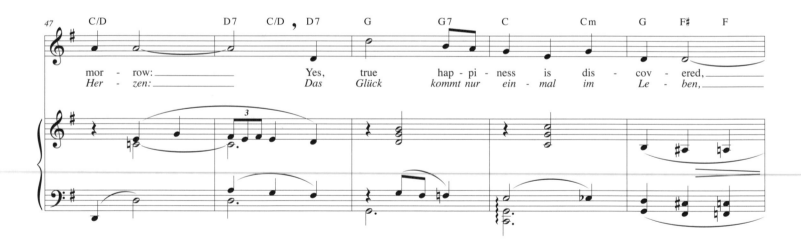

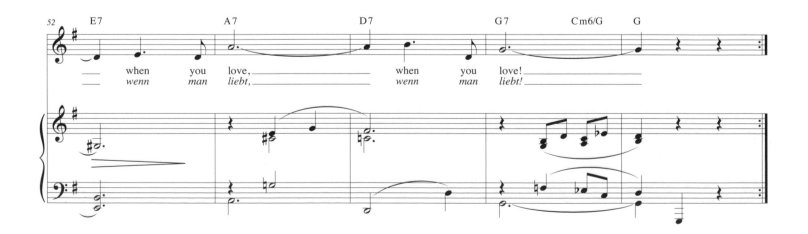

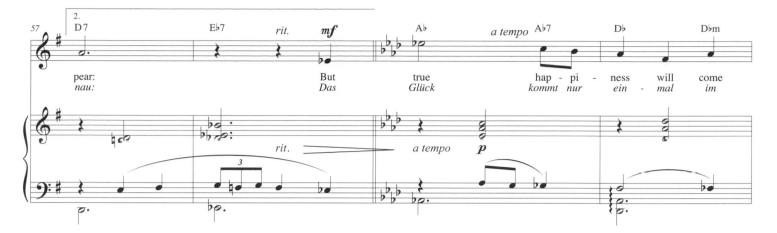

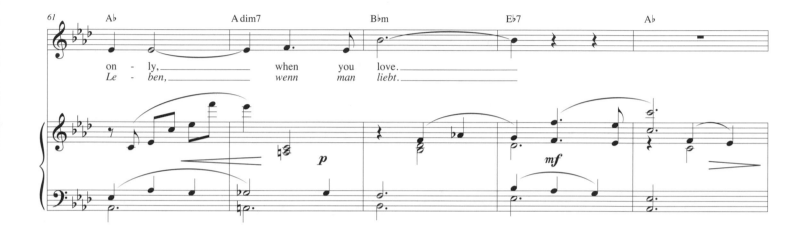

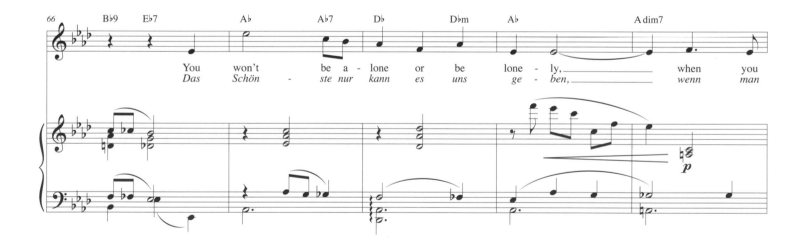

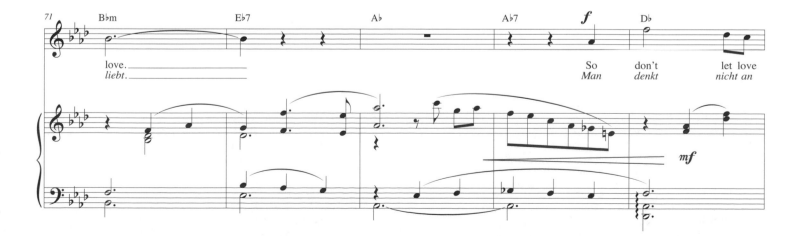

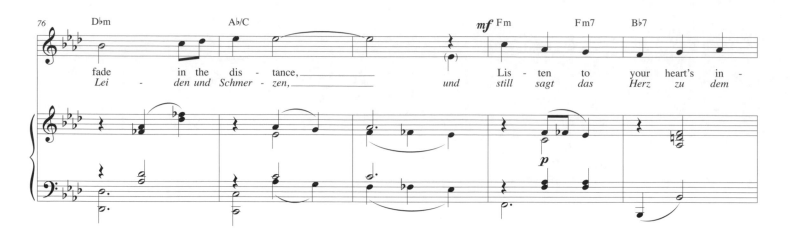

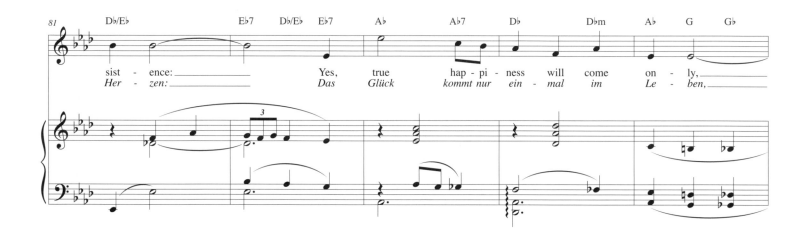

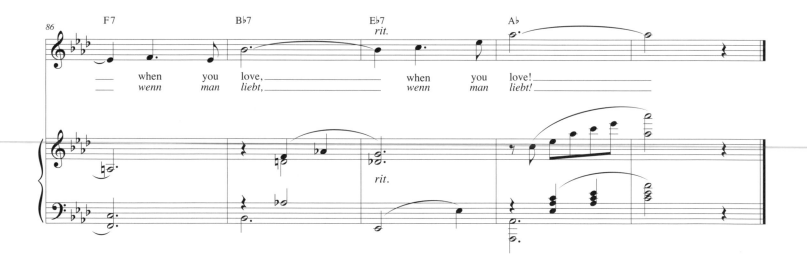

2. Even devotion, filled with emotion,
   sometimes will fail simply out of fear.
   Sometimes "I love you, think the world of you"
   can't make the sadness disappear:
   But true happiness will come only, when you love.
   You won't be alone or be lonely, when you love.
   So don't let love fade in the distance,
   Listen to your heart's insistence:
   Yes, true happiness will come only,
   when you love, when you love!

2. *Oftmals im Leben sagt man ergeben:*
   Du bist mein Glück, du geliebte Frau!
   Doch ist nach Stunden alles entschwunden,
   ist man allein und man fühlt genau:
   Das Glück kommt nur einmal im Leben, wenn man liebt.
   Das Schönste nur kann es uns geben, wenn man liebt.
   Man denkt nicht an Leiden und Schmerzen,
   und still sagt das Herz zu dem Herzen:
   Das Glück kommt nur einmal im Leben,
   wenn man liebt, wenn man liebt!

WHO WANTS LOVE

from the 1937 MGM film THE BRIDE WORE RED

Music by FRANZ WAXMAN
Lyrics by GUS KAHN

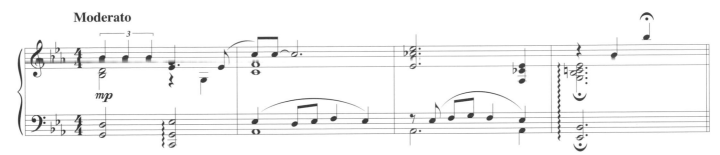

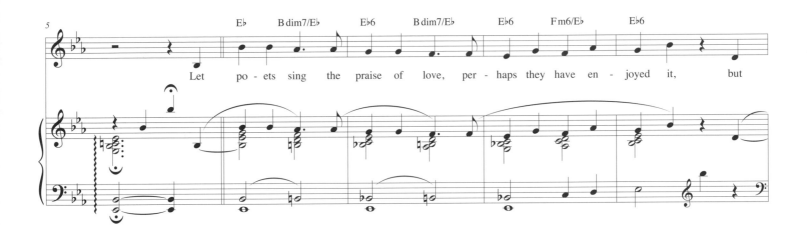

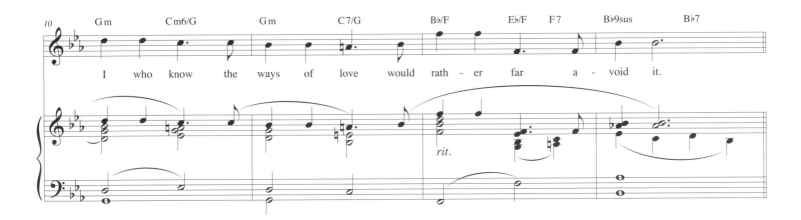

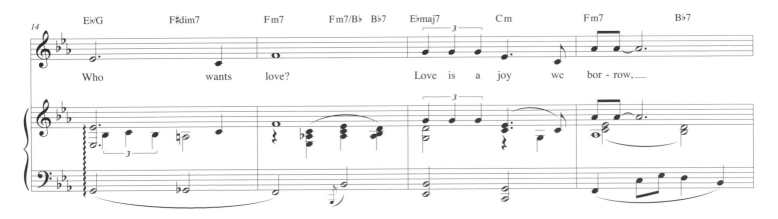

paid back in tears to-mor-row.__ So who wants love?

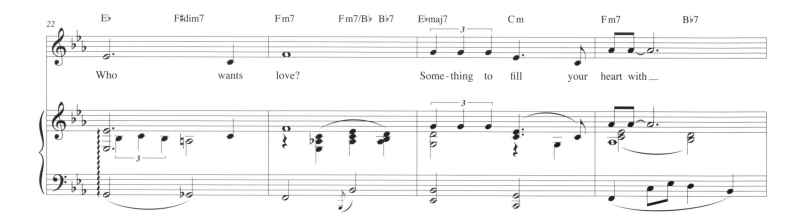

Who wants love? Some-thing to fill your heart with__

so ver-y soon to part with,__ so who wants love?

Love is a dream - er wear - ing moon-beams in pat - terns rare,

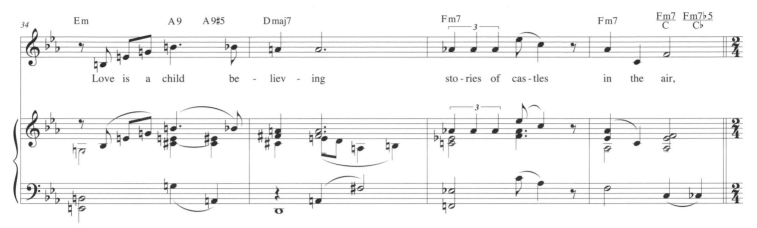

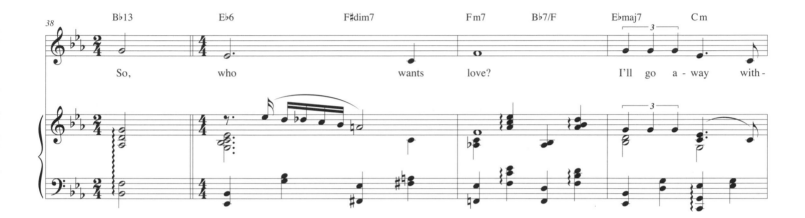

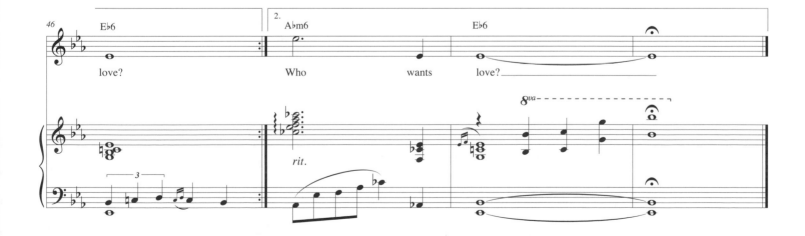

THE WISHING STAR

from the 1962 United Artists Picture TARAS BULBA

Music by FRANZ WAXMAN
Lyrics by MACK DAVID

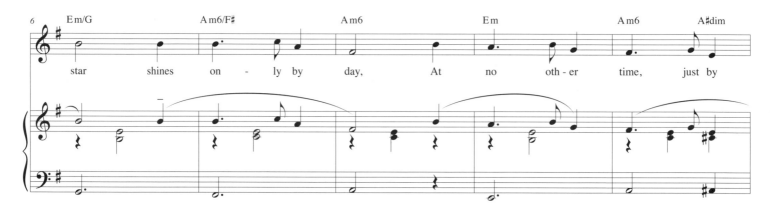

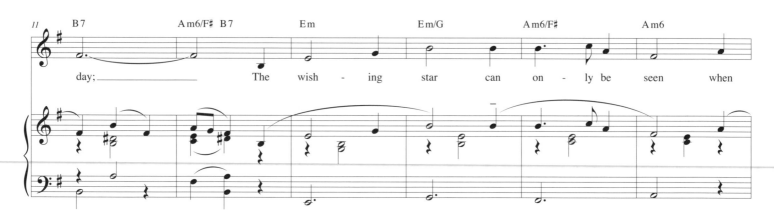

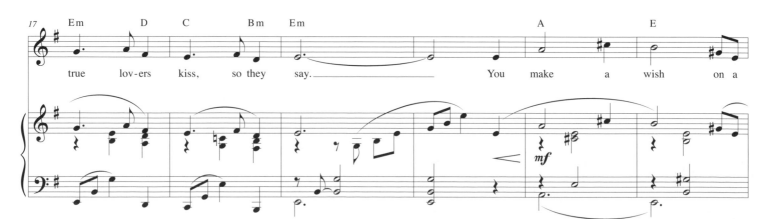

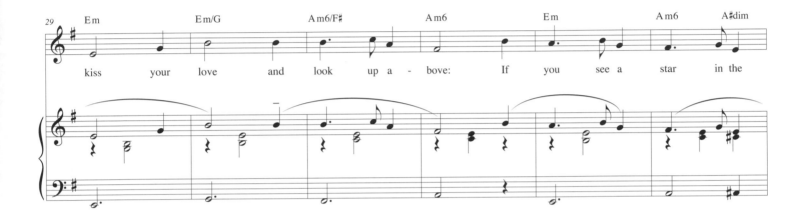

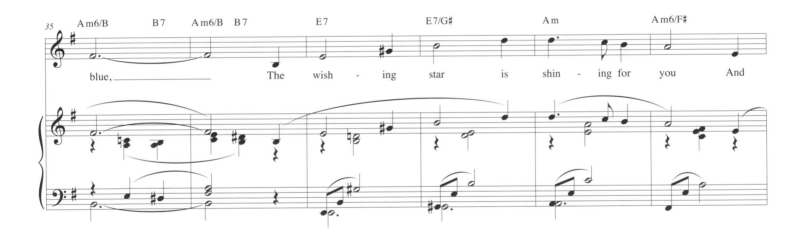

THE WONDERFUL SEASON OF LOVE

from the 1958 20th Century Fox Picture PEYTON PLACE

Music by FRANZ WAXMAN
Lyrics by PAUL FRANCIS WEBSTER

YOUNG IN HEART

from the 1938 United Artists Picture YOUNG IN HEART

Music by FRANZ WAXMAN
Lyrics by HARRY TOBIAS

Moderately (♩ = 70)

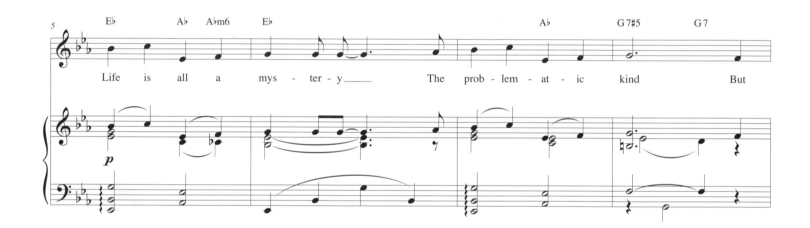

Life is all a mys - ter - y___ The prob - lem - at - ic kind But

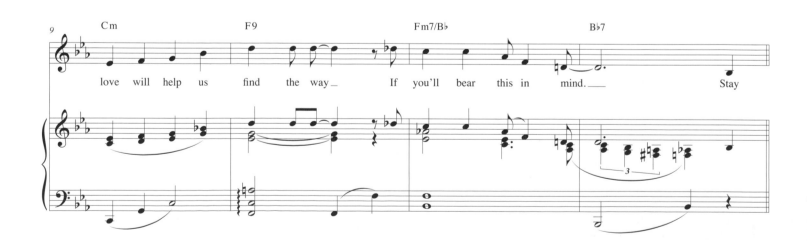

love will help us find the way___ If you'll bear this in mind.___ Stay

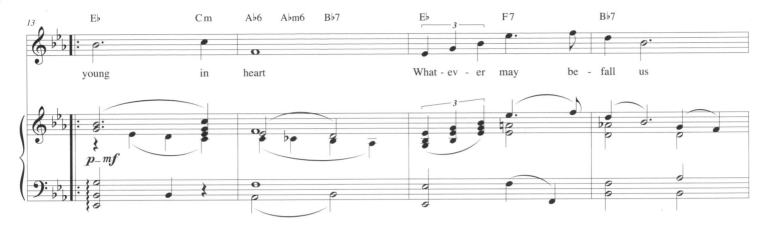

young in heart   What - ev - er may   be - fall us

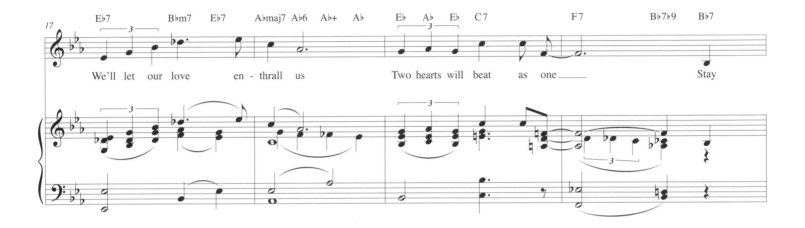

We'll let our love   en - thrall us   Two hearts will beat   as one____   Stay

young   in heart   You'll find your cares   are light - er   You'll see the fu - ture

bright - er   Bright as the morn - ing sun____   Time   brings man - y

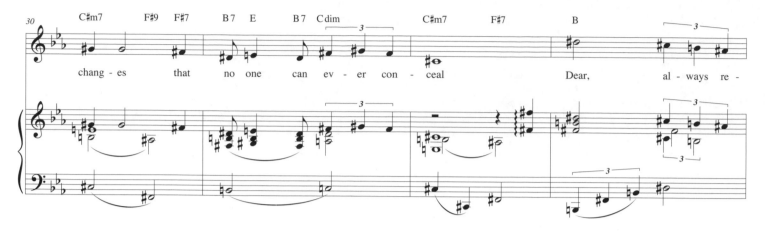

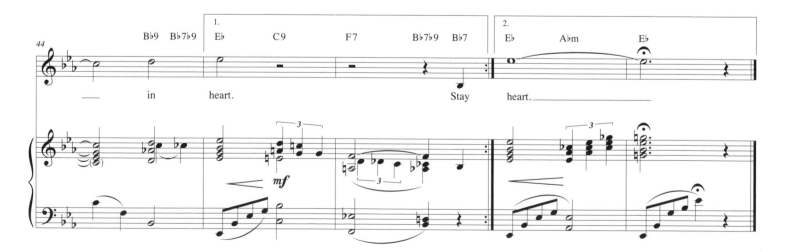